ELIZABETH KINCAID-EHLERS

LEAPING AND LOOMING

Merganser Press/Loon Publishing
West Hartford, CT
2005

Merganser Press/Loon Publishing
10 Fernbel Lane
West Hartford, CT 06107

ISBN 0-9766825-0-8

Book and cover design by Lisa M. Ciorciari
Cover photo by Elizabeth Kincaid-Ehlers
Author's photo by Drew Sanborn

Some of the poems in this collection first appeared in *Generation, The Trinity Review, Red Fox Review, The Connecticut River Review, Media, Northeast Magazine, The Hartford Advocate, Embers, Pudding Magazine, The Totem Pole, West Hartford News, Green Fuse, The Book of Other Virtues, The Daedalus Anthology of Kinky Verse, Living in West Hartford,* and in two sampler chapbooks, *River's Edge* and *Waterscapes*. "Mother's Day" was awarded first place in the North Country Poetry Contest (1996). "My Mother's Closet" was included in *The Anthology of New England Writers* (1997) and "Sailing Against the Wind" (as "Heading into the Wind") in *The Heartbeat of New England: An Anthology of Nature Poems* (2000). "Climbing Knocknarea to Queen Medb's Tomb," "Playing the bodhran along the way to Queen Medb's Tomb," and "Why I'm giving Jim the carved bear Steve has given me, maybe" were published in *Nimrod International Journal* (Spring/Summer 2001), and nominated for a Pushcart Prize.

Leaping and Looming

Collected Poems: 1979-2004

Author's Note

According to family legend, one day — on or about age three — I demanded that my mother stop what she was doing and write down my poem:

> Roses are red
> Violets are blue
> I love a cow
> Who gives milk and goes moo.

Since that time I have never stopped being badgered by lines, sometimes writing them down, occasionally putting them together and, once in a while, finishing poems. I have no relics from grammar school days; only published journalism survives from high school.

Even in college, in the cracks between papers and essays, I kept writing (there were also stories, pieces of novellas, and even chapters of novels). In 1953, at the end of my sophomore year at the University of Michigan, I won an undergraduate Hopwood award. To this day I remain proud of that honor.

In those days we wrote only formal poems: sonnets, sestinas, villanelles. The manuscript I submitted resides in the Hopwood Room, and I was able to get a copy, so I will include a few samples at the end of this note.

In my junior year, I married. After that things got complicated. I dropped out of school to follow my husband on his peregrinations. (I did go back to Ann Arbor to cram a senior year into one semester to finish my B.A.) All through the following years of beginning studies toward an M.A. only to have to abandon credits and move on; of bearing and raising children; and even, at last, of finishing M.A.'s and a Ph.D., most of the time while teaching, I kept writing. Not too long after the marriage ended, I moved on to a new life in Connecticut. Somehow, in all the uproar and confusion, the creative writings of the years between 1955 and 1979 were destroyed. So this collection contains only poetry from the twenty five years between 1979 and 2004.

And by the way: during one period in my early days in Connecticut, I ran around the state teaching writing in the schools. The idea was to give teachers help in learning how to teach creative writing. In one wonderful school in the northeastern corner, where I spent a blessed week, a fifth grade student interviewed me for the school paper. Although I had been introduced to her as Dr. Kincaid-Ehlers, in her published interview, she called me Doctor Kinky Waller: thus my irrepressible alter was finally named.

I remain grateful to my mother for the gift of language and the joy of reading. She would recite poems as well as read stories to me at bedtime. In my earliest years she also played guitar and sang old ballads that had traveled from

Scotland and Ireland to the Appalachians and into her bones. Her curiosity about other people's lives infected me, too.

To my father I am grateful for skepticism and one kind of intellectual curiosity. My saving humor comes from him, and to him I owe my outspokenness and an awful propensity toward defiance and argument.

I am indebted to too many teachers to name, to years' worth of helpful relatives, friends and even admirers, to students, particularly writing students, from the various universities where I taught, and to many clients, past and present. It was an intense pleasure to be invited by Rennie McQuilken and the Hillstead Museum to read as part of the Sunken Garden series. Finally, I was especially touched when the editors of *Nimrod International Journal* nominated three of my Irish poems for a Pushcart Prize.

This book would not exist without the staying power of my old friend, Louise Wheatley, and the kind competence of my new friend, Lisa Ciorciari. I would say I was speechless with gratitude, but they know me better than that. I thank them both.

And then there is the poetry group, without whom, not. A few other members have come and gone, but at the core are Susan Gimignani Lukas, whose moving away I have yet to forgive, and the stayers, Charles Darling, David Holdt, and Drew Sanborn. Without them, though I might have jotted on, I would not have finished and rewritten, and rewritten yet again. For their patience, fortitude, constancy and, yes, love, though they will not believe it, my gratitude goes beyond words.

Elizabeth Kincaid-Ehlers
West Hartford, CT
2005

ADDENDA

Here are two of the shorter poems from the Hopwood Contest entry manuscript. The entire collection was entitled, "Shattered Idols."

The Ancient Rite Of Parry

Since Love won't merely happen, you and I
Took something seeds from nothing; merged your
Tried soil with my potentiality,
And waited, watching, doing nothing more.
Then, wearying of watching naught,
We timed the while with ancient rite: thrust
Parry, parry and thrust as though we thought
By testing each to teach each other trust.
But now, since nothing has from something grown
You moan, lamenting death which you call crime,
While I, conceiving nothing to atone,
Grieve for a love miscarried out of time.
No, Love, your thrusting skill is not denied,
But this you did not kill, it merely died.

Yes, You May

Get up with the sun; fly with moon
Get drunk and sing a lewd new tune
And you may take two giant steps
Right into your grave.

Shirk at your work; pay for your play
Save time and better half that way
And you may take two giant steps
Right into your grave.

Sell out the old; buy up the new
Laugh at Death when he laughs at you
And you may take two giant steps
Right into your grave.

Fiddle dee dee; fiddle dee dee
Life is only a game you see
And you may take two giant steps
Right into your grave.

And here are two rondeaux, survivors of the years 1953 and 1954.

Ramification Of Benét
"Bury the by-gone South
Bury the minstrel with the honey mouth"

Honey Mouth, tell me who
Is by-gone minstrel if not you?
Who scorns the wormwood faces now,
Or sings to smooth the wretched brow
And laud with laud long overdue?
Who breaks with stars the barred taboo?
Who dares? The gloried past is through,
Perhaps it never was, so how
            Honey Mouth?
How sing what no one living knew?
The drums have beat a last tattoo
For one with courage to avow
A past the present won't allow
The by-gone; now we bury you,
            Honey Mouth.

Who But Elizabeth?

Who but Elizabeth, gentled so,
Allowed to live and probed to grow,
Would, kneaded soft, creep off to cry
And never think to wonder why
They treat a creature grieved to know
As though her brains were biscuit dough
And leave her lost, not knowing no,
To lie quiescent when they pry,
            Who but Elizabeth?
Who lives to loathe all life below
And poked and fingered full of woe,
Rolled until she will comply
Has let them bake her brains to die,
And stale, will in a crumble go,
            Who but Elizabeth?

Finally, here are the last six lines from a very long poem I wrote for my father in 1958 for his 53rd birthday. I was in Rome and mailed it home to him in Atlanta.

> ...Here is a man who knows today
> what he is doing; who has seen
> life as a wonder, and will say
> to those who care that he is one
> who lives an unspectacular way
> and is an ordinary man.

I found it saved with his important papers and documents after my mother's death in 1992. He had attached, in his own handwriting, a quote from Oscar Wilde:

> "children begin by loving their parents; as they grow
> older they judge them; sometimes they forgive them."

Now ask me if I cried.

to Theron, Quentin, Jordan and Morgan

for teaching me
much of what I know
about patience and love,
and for keeping me interested,
annoyed, impressed, and amused.

CONTENTS

FAMILY

FRIENDS

ODDS

ENDS

36

T178

FAMILY

My Mother's Closet

My mother's closet sloped.
Shoes mated in odd positions.
Boxes stacking the back wall
kept the eaves from plummeting
to the hard, narrow-boarded floor.
Afternoons, I drifted through the quiet
from one closet to another. Hers
was best; I could smell her there.
Stroking rayon, satin, silk, I nosed
around perfumed breasts of blouses
to collars where, on tiptoe, I could tuck
my head and dream. Turning my face away
from falsely scented seams,
I wrapped long sleeves around me.
Or, more rarely, I might squat
to try those troubling odors
in the places where her lap would be.
Oh, it was risky. I had been forbidden.
Getting caught was certain
and the consequence secure: pain, long
silence, then the ridicule. But I was a fool
for love, so I returned to kneel among
the tumbled buckles, straps and heels.
Shamed by deprivation, wondering
at my own dumb need, I pulled the surplice
of her skirts about me and sought some place
beyond. Detached from sadness, blame or anger,
I breathed my way back to my mother
until, in that imagined, motionless dark,
we were at one.

Mother's Day 1980

Birches clean and leaning light
the open woods of early spring.
Shadbush shines: somewhere shad
run in from the sea. Too late
for fiddle-heads, but here are pussy-toes
and shoots of white sweet clover.
Patches of trillium climb
low slopes of granite ridges
sharing dappled places
with pink spring beauty,
red-veined and edible. I nibble,
recalling violets in green salad
and my startled father. For amends
I made rhubarb pie. Next day,
ten years ago this week, he died.

May apple erupts, budded,
all parts poisonous save
the fully yellow fruit.
Wild lily-of-the-valley
poises for deadly bloom.
Though I know no harm of it
I will not eat this columbine
set to rocket into scarlet and gold.
Seeking liver-lobed hepatica
I chance on twin-leaf.
Shall I claim only what I can name?
Everything green announces itself.
He died because it was the season.
Sugars, fats, salts ran into his heart
where the years were waiting.

Elegant heron with terrible eye
turns toward a resonance of frog.
Redwings hang watchfully in the reeds.
Bullheads rise here, under waiting boats.
Across open channels in Grindstone Marsh
tree swallows, midnight and pale in the dusk,

open great mouths and fly pure miracles,
eating the evening. No mosquitoes yet,
only small flutterings of last light.
The last child, just ten, then
the baby they had come to see,
rides with me over the river
in the sunset cold and still.
I can do nothing for my mother now
except remember.

A Memory

She was three when her mother died
so make her five the year she went
to spend the summer on a big sister's farm,
safe, for a while, from the doctor's widow,
free, for a while, from the upstairs room.
The sister, nineteen or twenty years old,
had only a couple of kids back then
and time to sit in the afternoon,
to pick and sing and teach old songs,
to help small fingers twist the husks
and draw the face of her first doll.

Summer's end, she had to go,
along with the sister who was eight years old,
back to the crossroads town and the house
where the little girls fetched and washed and cleaned
for two step sisters and the wicked mother
who had married their father, the traveling man.
Whether he married up or she married down
never mattered to that littlest child.
At eighty six, what widened her eyes
was what made her say and say and say:
"she took my dolly and threw it away."

A Fable Of Babies

Once upon a time a baby came into this world
feared by her mother. When in the glare
of too much everything this baby caught the look
in her mother's eye, her spirit flew right back to Mars.

This baby's body was handled by men in bright white coats
and tended by women in bright white uniforms.
This much the baby remembers. Even watching
carefully she cannot see what happens next.

Once away from the hospital this baby is not fed.
Three weeks later she is taken back, starved nearly unto death.
Shifts of nursing sisters feed her. When she is nicely
plumped, they send her back to that same mother.

You cannot make sense of it. You might wonder
about the father -- she was said to be the apple of his eye --
and you might wonder about the aunts -- there were no grandparents
but there were aunts. You might even wonder about neighbors
or friends, but you will not make sense of it because that mother
starved this baby almost unto death -- again.

Back and forth she went: up she plumped
and down she starved -- again -- again -- again.

God's eye was on the sparrow.

When she was five months old this baby got pneumonia.
Everyone hovered around and at last the starving stopped.

This baby grew -- peculiar. She knows
that she is only one among the many babies
starved on earth. From Mars, where it remains
at peace, her spirit calls: "Every child
must be a wanted child," she says,
"and every baby born has to be fed.
What the gods do not notice, others must."
You can make sense of that.

Aunts

Aunts should live longer, long
enough to hear an old niece say
thank you, now I understand.

Mine are all gone, some long ago.
All are remembered. One is missed,
the one I am beseeching now.

That thing of sucking teeth, see,
it was not dentures, it was vacuuming
the gaps of serious gum disease.

Oh, Aunt, forgive my secret snickering.
I never forgot your whispering
the lifeline that I would be all right.

Nearing your dying time, when I accused
and said you knew and failed to rescue me
you never denied, just sighed,

said it had to come to this, apologized,
asked would I know how
to take a sister's child away?

Today I hear me suck my teeth,
and start to cry for my Aunt Mattye Belle.
May summers hold her gently.

I had no sisters. I do have sons. All
who whispered lifelines to them, take
my thanks. Aunt Mattye, take my hand.

In The Beginning

As the belt comes down
again again again
he quotes the Bible at her
in his Father voice.
He tells her of Jezebel
the bad whore Queen
whose body when they finally
stone it is so foul
the dogs will eat it not.

She wonders what Danny's father
is doing to him right now.
His mother tells on him the way
her mother tells on her.
He is almost five: "Wait
'til your father comes home."

She has been in her room
all afternoon. When he
comes in, clicking her door
behind him, and says,
in his German voice,
"You know you must be punished,"
she pulls her panties down
and bends over, waiting.

The belt comes harder and harder.
Finally she breaks and cries.
Now he can stop and comfort her,
sit down on her bed, whisper
in his Daddy voice, "I know you are sorry
for what you did. You will not do it again."

When she tries to move away
he drops kisses on her long, soft hair.
"Like my sister's," he says
in his smiling voice, "I know
you love your Daddy."

He starts to leave her room,
turns back and says in his business voice,

9

"You will not bother your mother
with fear that Beelzebub will get you.
Stay away from Danny. You understand."

After he leaves she pulls her panties
back up, and stands at her window,
looking out, wondering about that word:
Beelzebub.

Good News

My father comes home, sits, reads
his daily news. I want him to talk to me.
If I tap on his knee he will smack my
head. I am three. I know a thing or two.

> *She knew, and knew she*
> *knew, before lacerating lights,*
> *scarring voices on unbearable skin,*
> *the look in her mother's eye.*

I stand quietly watching paper turn.
Then the black marks jump.
I can see that they are talking to me.
I know not to tell. In secret I am reading.

> *Like volunteers with blue lights*
> *and shouting sirens, words had come*
> *to rescue her; taking her up to*
> *language, which became her one true home.*

Family Picture 1936

picnic on a sandy river bank

Observer: They smile to keep their mother happy,
      smile to keep their father safe,
      smile to keep from screaming,
      or maybe one of them is really fine.

Father: June in Washtenaw County
      Temperature (Fahrenheit) 68 degrees
      this event recorded on Kodak ASA 100
      aperature f8, speed 125
      all time is borrowed
      why eat sand?

Mother: Sun, take me now.
      I have done as
      I am supposed to do:
      the man;
      the handsome boy;
      the girl;
      house clean;
      weight 120 pounds;
      a hot meal in our picnic basket.
      I tried to be a good girl,
      would have loved my mother.

Boy	Girl
I want to be a good boy,	Here by the Huron, water low,
a good boy, a good boy,	brown sand warm,
I want to be a good boy,	-- must not say --
just like Dad.	play with the sauce pot, stir sand,
My sister is a bad girl,	remember scraping grit.
a bad girl, a bad girl,	Never love the river.
my sister is a bad girl	Let it move on. Move on

Dr. Kinky Waller Is Grateful To Certain Primary School Students In Rocky Hill, Connecticut

She tells the children
"you can write --
choose something that
you care about."
Sitting with them,
trying to find
the years between,
she sees the front porch
and hears, from
behind the big tree
in the back field
where she is hiding,
rising in extraordinary light
over ordinary houses,
the familiar voice
of her mother
calling her home.

Kinky Waller's Mother Goes Bye Bye For Good

When her mother dies
Kinky laughs and laughs.
All those years
stomping on cracks
pay off.
Not that she dies
of a broken back,
just that her heart stops.
Kinky stops to think.
She had not known
her mother had one.
Now Kinky cries and cries.

Father Christmas

One Christmas eve, too old for foolery,
I listened to the creak and pause
of my father limping down the stairs.
With accurate ears, I followed
his progress, imagining how my sock
would hang, over-long and oddly fat,
toe sagging, stuffed with one silver dollar,
arch swollen by an orange.

I know I heard him drink the Coke
and eat the pecan cookies that
we in the South left for Santa Claus.
Then he crept up, paused, passed
my door, and went to bed.

Awake with tricky energy
I watched night change among camellia
thickets and gardenia bushes
tangled under oaks and tall slash pines.
Toward morning, I snuck down myself,
put milk and crackers on the mantle,
and wrote a second note.

In later years, we visited or wrote,
teasing, trading jokes. If, in a quiet
moment, I would try to solve
the mystery of that Christmas, he would
mime a bafflement sober as my own.
What, he would ask, did I want?
I wanted to know how he did it.
When I so soon descended to lift
my stocking from its hook, the milk
was gone from the filmy glass, the Saltines
gone from the plate. On the note an
added line said "Thanks a lot, S. Claus."

I had thought I had you, Daddy.
In the end you slipped by me
one last time, dropping alone
into the darkness below the bottom
of the stairs, leaving me breathless,
waiting, still silent behind a closed door.

Shoe Shine Girl

Yes, it was another time, and things
were different then. My parents called
themselves careful, and were frugal.
We had chores and did them, complaining
quietly, if at all, and no slamming doors.
On Saturday morning I cleaned my room,
the bathroom and the stairs. I would
have preferred mowing the lawn
but girls were not allowed. Yet,
explain to me this: my father paid
a dime a pair for a good shoe shine
and I got the job so I made
30 cents a week in no time at all
polishing already spiffy business shoes
and for that he was proud of me.

Fiscal Responsibility

Once, as I was complaining again
about the money we did not have
he told one of his rare stories.
In 1913, when he was eight,
the youngest by far of six children,
he was called home one day from
playing ball in West Alexandria, Ohio,
which was largely German still
before the First War altered everything.
His mother gave him a nickel for bread.

The store was near the ball field.
He had come all the way back and now
had to go, come back and go again.
"Why can't we charge like everyone else?"
he whined, throwing the nickel down.

Spring in Western Ohio is wet
and muddy and so was my father
when he finally found the coin,
went to the store, got the bread,
paid for the bread, brought the bread
back to his mother, went to his father's
store, told him what he had done,
got his whipping, and went back to play.
At the end of the month, children from families
who charged their groceries were rewarded
with candy when the bills were paid.
My father's people paid cash and
their children received no sweets.

"But, Daddy, that's not fair," cry I.
And he? "Well, that is how it is.
We pay cash and what we do not need
we do without. What we need we earn."

More Fiscal Responsibility

The only loan my father shouldered
that I knew of was a mortgage.
In my memory they stopped renting
and bought a house on East Park Drive
in Midland, Michigan. I can go
there in my mind, the wide front steps,
the side door that we really used --
my room, my mother's closet, the cellar
where I hid evidence of my worst crimes.
Sometimes my father sat at table
long into the night, looking at papers.
His head in one hand, with the other
he made tall towers of numbers, sighing,
shifting a little, adding on.
I would worry about him, try
to pat his shoulder. He would say
"just run along. Go help your mother."

Botswana And Toccoa

Looking at a map in the world
section of the local paper,
full of the bliss of morning, I see
Botswana has the only case
of polio from coast to coast
in all its region of Africa. So,
it begins again. The sly
virus edges in by mouth,
slithers silently into the brain,
takes up lodging, evicts the nerves,
shuts down communication
until muscles, undirected, quit.

Oh, I know. I've learned the answer
to why me? is still why not?
In the small town of Toccoa, Georgia,
just below the Carolinas,
under Chatooga Ridge,
in the summer of '48,
all alone for fifty miles
in all directions, I was the only
one brought down.
And so it began for me.

They say of life's hard questions
if you cannot tell the difference
what difference does it make? It made
a difference then and makes one still.
Sometime this month, between the transit
of Venus and the penetration
of Saturn's rings, I suddenly had
to begin wearing glasses all the time.
One eye is closing down. That's just
the latest. Before this, my back
and knees and gut gave out
with different styles of breakdown.
These hands no longer garden and
this heart, though steadied, will not climb again.

My youngest says when he is slumping
all he has to do is take a shower.

What does he know of the deeps, that
place, prehistory, where there is no
geology, just magma at the core?

Now, reading the paper sucks
me into the dark where this world
no longer matters. No light.
No more believing. So I limp
in beneath the sounding waters,
reach blindly for the hopeful soap,
and wash my way to something,
what I cannot say.
I am here
and there is a here
and there is an I to be.

If we last the day
I will remember
to call and thank him.

Daddy Drives Home

Remember when
you drove up to Toccoa
to bring me home?
Imagine -- the phone call:
"Sir,
we have your daughter
here in the hospital
with poliomyelitis."

They curled me up on the passenger seat,
my head on your gas-and-brake leg.
The camp director threw my stuff
in back, waved us off. He had
to go inform all parents, close the camp.

In those days,
polio
stopped
summer
cold.

The thing is,
you were a heavy smoker.
Your lighter lay pocketed under me.
You drove
three hours south
to Grady Hospital
in Atlanta
with only thoughts
for solace:
you would not disturb my head.

Picture -- Blown Up

Someone, one of the guys, snapped
it from behind with the kind of Brownie
everyone had then, my father
standing in woods beside a lake.
Beside a river. Wherever they were,
some place in the Upper Peninsula
with boats and poles and skinny, tall trees.
He is off to the left, which he never was,
one arm propping up the other, one hand
holding the pipe he only smoked
while trying to quit cigarettes.
The pipe smelled better.
He looks trim, dapper under a regular hat.
I mean not a fishing hat, or cowboy,
just the everyday one he wore to work,
only there he is under a spruce,
little spruces springing up
around him, watching an outboard go by.
Mother had the print enlarged, framed
and sealed. Eventually she hung it
on the porch in Buckhead, Georgia,
where I would stare and stare, trying
to remember Michigan, where I
was little and nights were cool.
I have that picture now above my desk.
He keeps his back turned, still.

Sudden Bouquets

Sometimes, a surprise,
roses arrive at the office
for a secretary from her son.
Memories come like that.
My father and I, playing
with nonsense, chanting "oh
am she went and are she gone
and leave I all alone" --
by now both laughing
as all around us grow annoyed --
"oh cruel fate you is unkind
to take her fore and leave I hind
it cannot was." Daddy,
you died too soon.

Father Perpetual

Certain afternoons he is there
up in a corner of my office,
as though I could see him
looking down, not just in contempt
but with some genuine concern:
"What, exactly, do you
think you are doing here?"
Whatever client is there may
pick up on my distraction
but for the moment I do not know,
do not believe I have a right,
am sure I should have known
better in the first place.
I want to cry.
What I thought I was doing
was helping troubled girls
get over their father's harm.
"I teach them, Father," I think.
"I teach them to live a life
for themselves that makes
sense for them," I say.
"I help them give themselves
the love they need." "Nonsense,"
comes down from above.
"You coddle and you spoil.
Tell them 'get up' and 'get on
with it.' Shame."
I do not cry. I go on
with what I was doing.
We go on differently now.

The Dancers
A Narrative In Blank Verse

Saturday nights they transformed out of small
town bungalow people who turned collars
or said "yes, sir" at work into Fred
and Ginger or another magic movie couple
or even the luminous moving colors of Renoir.
So unlikely. They were both orphans,
making themselves up as they went along.
My mother lived for those few hours. My father
had to step up and step out, limp and all.
I liked them best, then, when they were too
much in love to care what I had done
or failed to do or might be about to ruin.

When my father died my mother tried
to keep on living. After a long while
she even went to sea on a monied cruise,
took up with the handsome boy singer,
spun on with him after the boat had docked.
Her sisters disapproved and so she stopped.
Thereafter she rode the same cab every week
to dance with gay young men at Arthur Murray.
Soon they vied to dip and turn with her:
the slightest hint and she would respond.

Meanwhile, since she could not think about
the disposition of my father's ashes,
I had taken them to Western Ohio
and put them under the stone prepared for him
by his mother in 1915 or thereabouts.
When the last of her five regular children died
only my father, the mid-life surprise, remained.
Just in case, she claimed a spot for him.
She died soon after, so I never knew her,
but I had been taken to see that waiting stone.
It haunted me. I think it haunted him.
I know each day was more than he expected.

At last, my mother had to end the "lessons."
Partners had begged her to dance with them in New York
in national competitions. The clothes, the hair,
the shoes, the fingernails -- she said no.

Only the dancing mattered, not a prize.
Sixty years of smoking stole her breath,
stopped her. She sat and waited and finally died.

So I had her ashes. What to do?
No final instructions. No hints. No *caveats*.
I asked the custodian in West Alexandria
to retrieve my father's ashes and send them back,
brought my mother's up from Atlanta,
and took them both to the famous crematory
at Cedar Hill in Hartford, Connecticut.
There with old-time courtesy, in a special
blender, a young man put them back together,
bade me watch. A fine dust rose, twirling,
and I knew they danced as one once again.

Their blended ashes sat on closet shelves
through many moves over years and years.
I was not bothered until my own heart jumped
a beat or two and lists of things to finish
lined up in my head. Then I remembered
how they had loved their one big vacation
(not counting the honeymoon they finally got
in the three weeks between retirement and death)
the year after Hawaii achieved statehood,
walking quiet beaches on western Maui
by day, dancing the evening into night
in the ballroom of the landmark hotel.
I knew where to go and what to do.

On what was truly a dark and stormy night,
undetected, I strolled the hotel grounds,
passed the building, went out to the end.
Legend has it that pu'u keka'a,
Maui's westernmost point, is the very
place from which spirits of the dead
leap into the unknown to be caught
and carried back to their ancestral home.
Alone in black and thunder I opened the velvet
bag, the heavy special box, and freed
my mother and my father, ashes and spirits,
watching as lightning showed the way for them
to dance together ever on and on.

A Habit of Love

In a small Northern company town
the plant is everything. No one
protests anything, not even
black slime chuting into the river
or chemical ash blackening
children's faces as they play.

Almost everyone has come from
somewhere else, some place
as white as this, with fewer
stores, perhaps, and
more foreign language.

Each week her father drives her
to Church and Sunday School,
his overcoat-over-pajamas
and management hat meant
to blind the watchers.
Each week, three hours later,
dressed, he returns to pick her up.

Under Northern pines behind
the gray stone church, a trailer
shelters the only black couple
in the county. Sneaking out in
resistance, once, she finds them.
Now each week, when her father
lets her out, she slips around to
the back, and they take her in.

White skin and all they
tolerate her, talking, leaning,
touching, following. Thus
she is hooked, so nothing
will ever change her.

Growing up she dreams of Belafonte,
Poitier, Freeman and Denzel. In

loneliness she longs for Butterfly,
Ethel, Mahalia and Lucille.

Back in the trailer she called them
Mister and Missus Brown.
All the rest of her life
she will call them home.

An Incident In Georgia In 1948

I. What she remembers and what she cannot forget

She remembers
the big black woman
slowly leaving the downtown bus.
She remembers watching her
start to cross in front of the bus,
the green light drawing her on.
She remembers seeing
the black-and-white coming fast,
flashers blinking without a sound.
She remembers knowing
what was going to happen
and watching while it did.

What she cannot forget
is the slow stately rising
of that big black woman,
her flawless silent spinning
in the bright Atlanta air,
her decent steady falling
headfirst toward the waiting road.

What she cannot forget
is the silence of no siren
and no braking sounds,
the cracking crunch
of the squad car's tackle,
the squash of the skull
meeting itself on Peachtree Street.

What she cannot forget
are the oranges
arced from their bag
in a high fireworks spray,
free at last from the juggler's arms,
spinning in sunbright orbit
until gravity catches them, too,
and they drop in a catchy rhythm

of random soft plops
beside the big black woman's
quiet body.

2. What she has not forgiven

Now this child watching
is white and a girl,
and still she knows
how this death will be hushed up.
Jumping off the bus she tells
the police, "I am a witness."
"You best get on home, girl.
Don't you mess in this."
"Write my name down," she says.
"I am a witness."
By now police are everywhere.
Some of them take her home.

"You keep this girl at home.
and out of our business,"
they warn her father,
who says very little:
he is from Ohio, his accent suspect.
After he smoothes them away,
he tells her "Do not rock the boat."
"But, Daddy, I am a witness.
I have to testify." "Mind me,"
he says, and turns away.

She goes up to the Cathedral,
her high Episcopal home,
to talk to the Young People's Canon:
"I am a witness, help me."
"Hush," he says, "mind your father.
You are still a child. Go home.
Pray for her soul."

A long time after,
on an inside page,
she finds a few lines stating

the city has paid a family --
nameless, no address --
funeral expenses for
an unavoidable demise.

3. What happened next.

It was still 1948
and this girl was still fifteen.
Perhaps she was no crazier
than she had been before.

But something happened.

She started integrating
busses all by herself.
No one wanted her to do it.
Drivers stopped, cursed,
threatened, threw her off.
Police picked her up, ungently,
hauled her home.
Her father took away everything,
grounded her for life.
Still, she went to school
and then to work
and with no warning
was compelled to stroll to the back of the bus
and sit and wait.
Even the terror in black women's eyes
would not deter her.

Of course it did no good.
She could see that nothing changed.
As she got older, police threats
changed from "We're going to get
your Daddy" to "We know
how to fix you, girl."
At seventeen she went
north to college.

In 1955, when
Rosa Parks refused

to move to the back of the bus,
this white woman's tears
could finally testify.

4. Additional consequences

Truth to tell, this girl
already fought for causes
before she sat on that bus.
Probably nothing else followed
from the moment she sat there
helpless to stop what happened.

Still, after all these years,
troubled at night, she'll see
that silent flasher flashing,
watch the oranges gaily rise,
hear the crack,
the thunk,
the plopping,
and, always,
never forget.

> "People long for justice, you know"
> Myrlie Evers, *NYT*, 11/27/94

M.L.K.

At a motel in Memphis
Martin fell
and took hope with him.

Jack was the shock
that popped the bubble,
Bobby the nail, the three, the out,

but Mister Doctor Reverend King
when he went down
he took hope with him

and some of us
never
got it back.

Romance In April In South Africa: 1985

"Men have died from time to time, and worms have eaten them,
but not for love..." Wm. Shakespeare, *As You Like It*

Here is Bontrug, black town
in the Eastern Cape
of white South Africa.

Here are young men
rowdy for human rights,
fired up for freedom.

Here is a young woman,
mother of three,
classified colored.

Black young men look
for brown woman's man:
she will not tell.

Black male hands
splash gasoline
on brown female skin.

Look! She burns for freedom!
Torches her own home
and shy, colored children.

The boy of seven burns fiercely;
the girl of six flames bright:
the baby burns right up.

Here, near Port Elizabeth,
in April 1985,
somebody died for love.

Watch Hill, Rhode Island
Easter 1980

Swan and osprey and a good, hard wind:
someone with conscience gets the Audubon Society
to guard this bit of pond, these tattered dunes,
and lets us walk here. We straggle over a golf course.
None of us plays, or wants to,
yet we keep off the green, proper citizens
come to see the ocean. Even our dog is leashed.

The boys are uniform in denim, denim and denim,
differing only in headgear: engineer cap, striped;
Australian bush hat, brim pinned with trout fly;
sweatshirt hood, pulled up, pointed, puckered.
Could I, thickened hippie throwback, gray hair long,
long past the fashion, pacify this little spit
hooking Atlantic to Long Island Sound?

No fossils, no flint chips, no Spanish coin.
Styrofoam lobster pot bouys, relics
that do not interest us. Only a few stones,
rounded in grinding undertow, pull us down
to palm them, rock eggs for the turning season.

When the high water mark encounters
a sea wall, we trespass: owners, we invite you
to visit our own watery places,
Sagadahoc Bay, or the islands
off the front of Leeds and Lansdowne.

Just off shore, mergansers surf and dive:
three pair red-breasted, one pair hooded.
Watched, their rakehell heads, crests and patterns
accounted for, they begin to look like decoys.
Wildness rises. An insurrection of peepers.

Loose dogs guard the lighthouse.

We should have revolution.

This scene not frozen yet,
for this year I will accept
this steady sea, this light,
this resurrection.

One Can Always Play Tela
(pronounced tay-la)

To win at tela you must place
your counters at three points along a line.
Both players start with nine,
taking turns at placement
as in tac tac toe.

Stuck again with a restless child,
feverish, flu struck, bored,
I think of other afternoons,
evenings when time clotted.
I remember days at sea,
the *Maria Teresa G,*
Giovanni Viganno, commanding.
The only piece of supercargo
on a small freighter
with a young crew,
I was twenty-two and running.
Three days out of Montreal
and trouble already,
the captain named me
sole keep of the chief engineer,
the only other older man aboard.
We sat, the Chief and I, eating
enormous dinners in the small saloon,
speaking of world affairs --
he with mechanical English,
I with grammatical phrases
about the pen of my aunt.
"Allora, Signorina," he would sigh.
"Signore, no," I would correct him:
"You must say *Signora*
for I am married
and entitled to respect."
Brooding over this American plum
consigning herself toward
the fruitpickers of aging Rome,
he fidgeted, groaned, sighed again.
"E, be'," he finally said,
"one can always play tela."
Stars in portholes

shuddering up and down,
he taught me how.

> *Each time you make a line you take*
> *a counter from your enemy,*
> *or from your friend*
> *if you should play with friends.*
> *Diagonals are forbidden.*

Now in this rented house
I half tend my child,
half attend to the past,
absorbed in what is lost.
"Tell you what," I say,
with blurring cheer,
"We'll play a game."

> *When all counters have been placed*
> *the game begins, unless*
> *it is already over, one player*
> *having lost too much to win.*

Brown eyes watch.
Nine games and two Cokes later,
catching me gone,
he wins.

> *To play, you move along the lines*
> *from point to point,*
> *maneuvering for the break --*
> *the opponent's mistake --*
> *the chance to make another row.*

Nine months after I first curved
around the Lugurian coast
my ingenuity expired.
Weeks of marked-down, greenish cheeses
and soft, spoiled oranges
led me running to the Embassy.
My parents said I'd made my bed,
my husband paid the fare.
Ten minutes after disembarking

I was pregnant. March it was, or April.
Jobless, we went home for summer.

> *Counters safely in a line*
> *cannot be taken. You must move*
> *and cannot occupy another's space.*
> *One of you will be trapped;*
> *breaking out of line, you will be taken.*

Something was wrong.
Our old family doctor,
probing my mysteries,
announced a big mistake:
"No baby there," he said.
My parents, prompt to take in labels
for their wayward child, adopted
false pregnancy and whispered.
My husband took to sleeping
in my brother's old bed.
I sprawled, sore-breasted,
tender-bellied, in the hot Georgia sun.
The meager ryegrass lawn still verged
on a creek grown over with creeper
and secret with water moccasins. No one
ventured into the chigger-dense,
dark wood. My body waited.

> *Malignant players insist upon*
> *defeating all the pieces.*
> *Refusing all concession,*
> *they remove them, one by one.*

> *We have a board, wide spruce, with points*
> *and lines indelibly incised, and hand-cut*
> *wooden pieces, nine cubes, nine disks.*
> *But you can rule concentric squares*
> *on paper, and gather sets of things:*
> *coins are nice, new pennies and new dimes.*

On a steamy Sunday in July
came the backache I'd been waiting for.
It was as though I had always known
how the cramps would crescendo
through the long afternoon;
how I'd clamp my teeth and shudder

while my pelvic cradle broke;
how the leaking pink would thicken
by the time I locked myself into the bathroom,
into clots big and black as fists;
how I would squat above a pie pan,
watched only by a scorpion
up from the drain for a look,
and grunt and strain
and contemplate my sins
until with a slither
that tiny *foetus*
would emerge;
how I would pack the gray remains
into a Peter Pan peanut butter jar,
sluice my thighs, wad a towel
between my legs, unlock the door
and tell the hovering trio
that something had from nothing come.
Or was it nothing come from something?
Though the pregnancy might have been false, the
abortion had been both spontaneous and true.
Earlier, feeling the afternoon attenuate
with the first tightening in my lower spine,
I had set up my table, got out my board,
found my pieces, roused my husband,
and laid my counters down.
One can always play tela.

Getting Through The Night

Often these days with Emmy Lou, playing
"every time you leave you tear the soul
from me," over and over 'til the tape breaks
and I must buy a new one.

Sometimes The Seldom Scene, John Starling, raised
by the railroad tracks, seeking, promising "some of us
find." Or my Uncle Bradley, riding on ahead,
his hand upon the throttle, his eye on the rail.

Mostly it's Emmy Lou, promising it
will soon be all over, cut and dried, though I
still "have this urge to go all bottled up inside."

It could be Kelly Willis, another gypsy,
born howling on the mountain side,
tracking through my mind.

Or the birthday tape my son made of
lonely mothers dreaming they hear the children
on the porch when it's only the wind.

Still I come back to Emmy Lou, walking
to Birmingham from Boulder, colder every night,
trying to see "if I could see your face."

These Days Kinky Stays At Home

These days
Kinky stays at home,
tries out chairs,
stares out windows.

Only sour necessity
draws her out --
garbage, bottles, cans.
Birds go unfed.

Dogs get fed.
Their scat piles up on the run.
They never get to run,
have almost quit howling.

Unemployment Compensation -- 1982
State of Connecticut Labor Department

Treating myself to a parking lot
I'm in line early today,
testing bioenergetic stances,
knees flexed, ready to spring.

    No big assaults this morning;
    no children pulling in hot despair
    at hand or leg; no lines swelling
    like sprinkled paper snakes
    from new lay-offs or closures.

Feet solid on the ground
I look up from the color of shame,
the lint of disintegrating lives,
to survey the ranked, ripped
vinyl and chrome of the waiting place.
No one yet too far behind.

    We are classless here,
    integrated, and often kind.
    Spanish has become so familiar
    I forget I never learned it.
    Black voices comfort like home.

Doing Yoga neck rolls
I feel less twitchy than the man
shooting his cuffs in the next line over.
Unfocussed eyes mark him a beginner.
A good boy all his life,
sharp, white and clean,
what can he make
of all this broken promise?

    One man, a runt with hungover stubble,
    shuffles out for a long harangue:
    "The god-damned women," he crows,
    "bringing the country down."
    Women let him back in line
    that he might collect his check.

The others in this enormous room
stay the far side of glass.

What keeps them doing what they do
except the fear of becoming what we are?

       Once I waited for five hours. Once I was sent back
       to the end of the line for failure to fill out forms.

Today in sweeps an oversleeper --
she has missed her appointed time.
Let her in. It is rainy and cold.
Have we earnestly looked for work this week?
Yes, sir; yes, ma'am; yes, boss.

       When I stopped swallowing rejection
       I stopped throwing up in the night.

To do Feldenkrais awareness-work
one should be lying down,
slowly turning the head from side to side,
doing the movement in the mind as well.

       Always the signs confuse; these lines
       divide according to the final digits
       of our federal identification numbers:
       these three are for extensions only;
       those are for new and re-applying;
       down there is out-of-town.

I think of words I would like to use:
epistemophilia, aubergine.
Except for grateful notes from former students
I would forget I ever taught.

       We must provide our own interpreters.
       When the man ahead cannot be understood
       they stand him to one side.
       How shall we connect?

Witnessed, I sign my name,
receive my check, my forms,
and my time for next time.
This young man seems new:
"Good luck," he says, softening
a piece of my obsidian heart.

       I feel my feet walking away.
       In the room still marked "Ladies"

I empty myself of whatever I took in,
then read a message:
   "Steve Dowling socks a mean pussycat
   (signed) "his wife and girlfriend"
I am not sure what it means.
Hope somewhere, someone
is keeping something up.

Reversals

On what would have been their 32nd wedding anniversary
except that he had left some time ago

She wanted the boys
to tussle like puppies
on a cabin floor,
grapple and pin
in fierce love,
trying out power
while they could still
be kept safe.
Sunlight licking
fair heads and dirty paws,
she would stand
at a black and nickle stove
stirring cornmeal mush
and humming in the morning.

In winter washed light
she keeps watch alone
in a kitchen smeared
with kibbled bits and mud
while two golden pups
squat over yesterday's news,
lurk, pounce and hurl
each other from sink
to pantry in terrific progress,
knocking down all things
moveable in this small flat
with high spirits and low cunning,
rough-housing just like boys.

Dr. Kinky Waller Addresses Diction And Grammar

Remember: Lie, lay, lain:
                           Lay, laid, laid.

I would lie
were I to tell you
that we never lay
where you and I had lain.

The bed still lying
north to south
as the land lies,
we lay watching moon
lay trail across water,
through rising grass
and over sill
to us lying still
north and south
as the land lay
and the boards had lain
when carpenters laid the floor.

When the moon lies fair
getting laid fits
all this parsing.
Each of you memorized
whichever breast lay
close to hand.
He laid his burdens down
just where you laid yours.
You lied first.
The past of lie is lay.

46

Buying A Second Gun
Part One Of An Unfinished Tale

The first one does not count.
Sitting up alone all night
reading *Perelandra*
terrified me into buying that one.

Richard, my absent husband's friend,
went across the water with me
and down the road to Watertown.
His years in the Marines
and the shrapnel in his feet
were equally commending.
We chose a Mossberg .22 calibre
seven-shot repeating rifle
with a clip.

Alone again that night
high on the island's ridge
in that isolated rented cabin
I read on, my gun across my knees,
peering periodically into the dark
with a quiet steady heart.

On that trip to town
Richard and I also bought
a seersucker suit for my husband,
who eventually returned
from wherever it was he had been.
I think he liked that suit.
At least he wore it for awhile,
instead of curling his lip
and throwing the clothes back into
the bag for me to return.
They say his present wife
is better at accommodating him.

All I ever shot with that Mossberg
were targets and my cat Kierkegaard.
Kierky taught me a lot. Then he
got distemper, giving up his
existential stance to climb walls.
I killed him with one shot. Before

I could let go the trigger, six more
cartridges poured through. By then
he was more dead than any cat had need to be.

My visiting father helped me
bury the remains. One of the few
agreements we ever reached was
that that cat was dead. Yet I had
tried to please my father. He hated
cats and so, the last I owned before
I left his house I had named "Dammit"
that Daddy could have at least one
pleasure sanctified: "Get out of my chair,
Dammit," he would yell,
giving my mother the look.

The upshot of that Mossberg
is a story I cannot tell.
We built a cabin just before
the marriage ended. The rifle
hung on pegs above the window
to the right of the sliding door.
The last I saw of it, one
of our sons had taken it down
and aimed it at another
in a dispute over which of them
would leave the island in
their father's mistress's boat.
I hid the rifle in a long tent bag
and never saw it again. No one
admits to knowing, and each believes
the other knows what happened
and is lying.

Art Tells Of Watching Kinky Make Tea

You should not be there
when she rips the tag off,
pinches the little string
and holds the bag out
over the scalding pot.

Do not witness
when the kettle screams
and she lets the boiling stream
leak just fast enough
to make that tea bag dance,
shifting with its every jerk
to keep those searing trickles
swelling the twitching tea.

When the pot is full,
the dangling tea bag
drowned and still,
the lid snapped tight,
Kinky will pour and drink.
Do not accept her offering,
not even for old time's sake.

Demeter

Since she could not
use the Greek
forbidden her, she
had to find another
way not to say
what she meant,
to tunnel rage
beneath her feet,
make it disappear,
come up dogwood,
each word bloody
on all sides, no
sentence strong
enough to kill
or die on.

Buying A Second Gun
Part Two Of An Unfinished Tale

When you leave
to find a missing father
in Parris Island, North Carolina,
I imagine discipline,
a little deprivation,
and lots of repetition,
so I throw a farewell party
and wave and wave
and wear a bright uplifted face.

Then you write,
telling of DI's forcing water
until vomit floods the decks,
and boot blisters oozing
the bright yellow pus
of infection nearing your bones.
At least I have learned enough
to pretend I <u>am</u> your father
when I call to send the Red Cross
to see about your feet.

You work hard, overcome great odds
to qualify as Expert Marksman,
able to kill how many people
I forget in just how short a time.
For prize, you are awarded
one brief call home.
I wait all weekend by the phone.
Days later, coming in from work,
I hear, in mechanical rasp
on my answering machine, "Mom,"
I wish you were there." The sound
that rips up out of me is a sound no
longer mine -- it is the sound of all
the mothers everywhere who forever
miss and lose their sons.

Buying A Second Gun
Part Three Of An Unfinished Tale

I should have risen at once
and marched
as we did in '64
and shouted
"Hell no, we won't go,
we won't die for Texaco"
but this is autumn 1990
and I love a son
who loves the Marines
and the sounds of men
smashing each other
on hard cold fields.

Twitching with what
you call drill dread
you wash, starch and iron,
neatly stow the strewn gear
and leave for Plainville
to fulfill your duty
to the Reserves.

Sunday night, you drag
up the stairs, boot weary, hungry,
cold and tired. "Ma, I'm sorry,
I have to do this," you say,
and hand to me your last
will and testament, dated,
witnessed and signed.
Sound-minded, you have left
all you have to me.
"The CO says we will probably go
before the end of the year."

We need more time
to squabble over
feeding the dogs,
taking out garbage;

time to figure out
what it is I have
to leave to you.

I read about my rights re:
the disposal of my veteran's
body, fold the document neatly
into the strong box next
to your birth certificate
and first shorn red-gold curl.

Quiet, silent in the terrible
stillness of rage and chronic prayer,
I choke on NO NEVER NOT
retire and rise to make you
oatmeal, wave you off to your local
college classes where you have
just begun to aim
both feet in one direction.

And then I cry.
All the mended places
in this shattered heart crack;
the tears of all those long,
long years arrive.

I pray to every anyone
or thing who might have power
to hear or care to act
or ever did:
Sun
Earth
Oak
Stars
Moon
Goddess
Wind
Rabbits
God
Turtles
Spirit
Planets
Bears
Saints
Rooks

Grass
Isis
Fate
Wolves
Fairies
Babies
Mary
Kali
Time

It is not right for a son
to die before his mother.

Three Things For Peter B.

I could bring you these:

> the name of a man who remembers the first
> 35,000 digits of *pi*;
>
> the word for the act of scattering stones
> on a field to hinder farming;
>
> the dream of a boy sent to fight in sand
> before he comes home again.

Kinky Sends Smoke Signals

Twitcher, one of Kinky's sons,
is restless on an island.
"Gotta go," he says, "gotta leave,
gotta get myself some smokes."

Kinky's ears grow pointed.
"If I chain you to this post," she asks,
"how long before you give it up,
relax and lose the itch?"

"No time at all," says Twitcher,
"I'll gnaw off my leg
and I'll be gone." Kinky
gets her camera -- and a chain.

Talking Incorrigible

She will go down chattering,
count on it, all syllables falling,
missing nothing even when
it is in her head.

Her sons will be suffering,
for certain, but peaceful, hearing
nothing, no constant commentary,
not a single word.

Once, along the Thruway, traveling,
she put signs together, saying
"Navajo Truck at Chittenango" until
they prayed just to get home.

Meeting Abbie
for Abbie

I warned my son not
to let us meet if he
and your mother did
not mean to keep together.
You were three already
and I knew my heart.

Child, I was cautious:
offered you a stuffed pup,
hoping you would take to me,
there, in the cabin at the River.
When you left, you went crying
over this new daddy's shoulder,
"Too sad, Grandma, too sad."

Meeting Abbie Again

Coming back to my old town
to greet your new-born sister,
I am sent with you on an errand.
Not my old neighborhood,
cold with encroaching dark.

Outside the corner store
I turn to go toward home
and lose your hand. You
have set yourself. I do not
like the stubborn on your face.

Strange streets, stranger people.
I try the grandmother bargain --
"We'll go Abbie's way awhile,
and then we will go mine."
You offer a silent hand

and lead me straight to the door.
Child, how did you do that?
Not yet four, already knowing
how to go out into the world,
turn, and go safely home again.

My Day Off

Comes the plumber who does not recall
his prior coming, claims a senior moment,
as they call forgetting now, but vows
to sort a refuse heap to find the fittings
that will keep these old pipes working, my
shower walls dry, the plaster in the room below
tight and white as it's supposed to be.
I choose submissions for a magazine,
routine and lacking hope, read the paper,
clip a grammar error for the file,
and save an article on dizziness
since it has just commenced to rattle me.
In town I run the usual errand route,
down Main to the bank, around the corner
to the Post Office and back across the green
to the Library main branch to pick up
interlibrary loans of poetry
and essays on writers' mental health.
Crossing Hartford on the highway I sigh
again at holes in all its possibilities,
check that Trinity's spires remain intact,
swing south along the river, pass the cove,
turn off at Rocky Hill and reach the Dive Shop
where I intend merely to get good gear
for Abbie and me so we can go snorkeling
on the islands of Hawaii, Maui and Oahu.
What I do not intend is to hear again
the sirens singing, feel the lure of the deep,
to come on pathetically to Tom the proprietor
so he will take me on his boat far away
to dive in deep blue water once before I die.

Letting Go
for Ashley

I tell Grandfather
how furious I am;
forty years drunk
and the drinker stops,
too late for us
and for the family
shattered, scarred.
Grandfather says
it doesn't matter.

I tell him my sons
run now to love their father --
it seems they don't look back.
Grandfather, I say,
I hate that parable,
the fatted calf,
the glad rejoicing.
Grandfather says
it doesn't matter.

My granddaughter,
losing something
that she wants,
says "that's okay"
and "that's okay."
I ask how long I'll suck
this bitter root.
Grandfather says
it doesn't matter.

Kinky Curses Cursive

Jill   Jill   Jill   Jill
Jilt   Jilt   Jilt   Jilt
Jet   Jet   Jet   Jet

Kinky's grandaughter's perfect rows
earn the biggest smiley faces.

Kinky always got the frowns.
She cursed the enterprise
before she knew the curses,
scribbled prior to the writing
and scribbled ever after.

Oh, she could print
humiliation's history:
notes home in perfect teacher's
perfect Palmer Method;
notes back in perfect mother's
perfect Appalachian hand.

Recalling bright red F's
effacing seas of little black A's
she thinks, "dear Jill, please
jet me out of here,"
but total recall is coming on

       jilt   jilt

the youngest child ever
required to type her school work

       jolt   jolt

professors pull her out of college classes
to break her own Rosetta codes
and shame of shames:
her graduate school committee
meeting in formal session
in the presence of God
and an outside examiner
requires her to read aloud

her stacks and stacks of blue books
from hours and hours of qualifying examinations
because none of those distinguished professors
can read a word of what she's written there.

Back then her letters home
were propped up on the mantlepiece
for passersby to take a flying guess at.
Now her notes away from home
stick on frigidaires
for sons to shrug
and finally give up on.

"Tomorrow," says Kinky's grandchild,
with magic lantern eyes,
"we learn **K**." Together
they think of kindly K words,
"keep" and "kilt" and "kangaroo."
Kinky hopes the child gets smiley
faces on her K words, too.

But Kinky thinks of other words
too harsh for second grade,
and with her finger fashions in the the air
illegible strings of "kick" and "kick" and "kick,"
and "KILL" "KILL" "KILL" "KILL" "KILL."

A Ceremony For Ashley Who Asked For One
When Bad Dreams Filled Her Dream Catcher

Early
while Sister Dew still decorates
Spider Woman's weaving
and shows the trails
of all night creature journeys,
rise,
dress warm and plainly,
go to an open place,
find rocks to make a small circle,
lay
cedar, sage and sweetgrass
in the center of the stones,
light
them with fire
to free their spirits
that they might rise
and take your prayers
to where Great Spirit
blows
beyond all winds.

Face
each direction --
East, South, West and North --
and thank it:
thank Father Sky
and Mother Earth
for being with you.
Thank all the ancestors
who came before:
ask blessings for all
who follow.

Thank all your relations:
the four-legged ones,
six-legged, and especially
the eight-legged people
who first taught us to weave.
Thank the fur-bearers,
the swimmers,

and the stone and fire people
who offer their spirits
to carry prayers for yours.
Ask them all to help you now.
Sprinkle
corn and wheat on the fire
to honor all the spirits
listening to your prayer.

Step
slowly around the circle
holding your dream catcher
by its cord;
move it back and forth
through the rising smoke
to the rhythm of your heart.
Ask wind and sun
to clean your web
that it might purify your dreams.
Honor any birds
who fly to help.

Honor
especially
the Spirit of the East,
the place of birth
and new beginnings.
Ask it to clean your web
and make it new,
so its power will protect
and its medicine heal you,
its energy keep watch
through all the long nights,
making dreams good for your life
even when they are sad,
or angry or frightening,
keeping you safe
from evil dreams
that would afflict your spirit
and turn you from your path.

Put out the fire.
Thank all the spirits
for being with you.

Hang the dream catcher
over your bed again.
Thank it for serving you well.
Ask it to keep on.

Then run out and laugh and play. Love, Grandmother Elizabeth,
Elder of the Woman's Lodge

P.S. Hey, Ash, ask your Mom or Dad to help with the fire stuff, ok?
I don't want you to get hurt, or either of us to get into trouble.
Thanks. love, Grandma

A Traveler's Tale

Slant light picks out a different palette,
reds, browns, the gray of Taos Mountain.
There, from the western *portal*, she sees the distance,
the monsoon shrouded sun ready to set,
ropes of dry rain hanging on their way
to farther peaks over the high plateau.
She has made it, fleeing in one day
from record touching Eastern humid heat
to this *casita* in New Mexico.

Self-absorbed as any child in wanting
what she wants, she gives it up when she
starts noticing, will lose herself in wind
shifts, sudden thunders, buzzards funneling
down on something small and dead out
on empty land beyond the graded road.
Jack rabbits leap and stop, swivel
ears, fade into rabbit brush, just
as they should. High, dry, silence.

Then it begins, a truck roar, gravel scratch.
Door slam. Loud voices. One deep, cursing.
A language she does not speak, yet understands.
Air so clear she hears slaps across the sand
and sage: blows echo, reverberate.
"Not mandated here," she thinks, "not bound,"
but cannot bear it. The landlady says, "please
do not report it. I'm the Anglo here.
My tires will be slashed, my burro injured."

"It happens every year, after Fiesta.
Always on Sunday when the drinking's done,
or Monday, when the good time's really gone."
So the traveler goes inside, shuts the windows, draws
the blinds, turns the T.V. on and finds
on PBS a farce where no one's hit,
no wife is kicked, no child wrenched and crying;
where everyone speaks flawless Oxford English,
and inebriates all fall comically down.

Strangers

*Hogmanay is the name for Scottish New Year. The saying is:
"if you can remember Hogmanay, you didn't have a good one."*

We happened to step in step
from the bagel place,
stop to see the blue-black
blue of a Pittsburgh evening,
hear a nighthawk's scree,
look up together, spot its
scimitar swoop and watch,
shoulders touching, sighing
in release of so much grace
and the night still coming on.
We turned, gave each other
our eyes and the light we needed,
parted with smiles and walked
away down different streets,
in those five minutes closer
than ever I was with my husband,
except for one long afternoon
on a Vancouver Island beach
where we sat side-by-side,
our children playing all around.

Telling this starts me cleaning
my house for Hogmanay.
That man in Pittsburgh
might have been first visitor,
the well of a fresh new life.
No. First-footer should be dark,
tall, lacking imperfection, the way
my husband seemed to be.
This man was reddish, like a Norseman
come to plunder along a coast.
I would have been throwing salt,
tying twiglets with red thread.
Even ritual gifts of bread and coal
with sprigs of evergreen
could not ward off such evil.
And then there was the *usquebaugh* --
water of life by the dram.

My husband certainly took
the sips. Such liquefaction

should have brought more luck.
Once started, it would rain
as though it rained upon
St. Swithin's Day, threatening
never, ever to stop. Someone
should have put him out to
have what Swithin wanted; rest
in a "vile, unworthy place
under the drip of eaves."
He, too, might have been
converted. Oh well, let's put
this house in order, let the old
year out. That red-haired man and I
can wish each other luck in the gathering
dark of Pittsburgh, then move on.
It is as good a way as any to go home.

Kinky Waller has a friend so slow
to learn Kinky doubts she will.

This woman practiced staying alive
until she got it right,
she thought,
and practiced loving
until she got it right,
she thought,
and practiced babies
until she got that right,
she thought.

But she had only boys
and they turned into men.
They get uneasy when she feels,
and more uneasy when they feel uneasy.
They will not practice feeling.

They stay away and tell her to.

Kinky tried to help her friend.
She offered knives and scissors:
"Cut the cord, cut the losses,
cut the line," she said.
"Cut a new deal, cut the melancholy,
cut the crap."

Her friend is listening,
almost hears it right,
she says.
She's practicing not caring,
almost sealed it tight,
she says.
But she keeps opening
a hand
fat full of softened heart.

Winning And Losing

In hopes of jogging her sagging brain alive
she enters the vocabulary bee at the local
Senior Center, where she wins the prize.

All should be well, but it is not. A word
she was not dealt and therefore did not miss
is now defined and she's forever lost.

She had thought that Salmagundi was
a place, a geographic locus west
of somewhere else, the island she would get to

when, at last, she organized her life.
In the contest, "salmagundi" meant
a mixture, an assortment, a potpourri.

At home she checked a lexicon and found
it meant a dish of gamebirds, minced and stewed,
or the spicy sauce where late the wild fowl sank.

Dr. Kinky Waller Fools Around With Words

A gynotikolobomassophile
is one who likes to nibble
on the lobes of female ears.
This makes one who fears
to risk the taste of manly lobe
an anthrotikolobomassophobe.

Prayer/Mantra

I am safe
I love and am loved
I am not alone

surely an early ape
wanted to feel this way
never mind if it
could form the thought

and all those starters
of one-god religions
in their hours of anguish
cried out the same

so as I sit in Quaker Meeting
asking blessings on children
seeking a home
all the while I intone

I am safe
I love and am loved
I am not alone

The Dump

Sir: This morning,
with the help of friends,
I took the last mattress
from the old days
and tossed it on
the Lansdowne Dump.

It was legal. I paid
ten dollars for ten
landfill stamps, enough
for the double bed size
<u>and</u> the foam mat we
had used to try to make
the marriage bed softer.

So. This much is done.
I will not have to think of it
or struggle not to any more.
To love the sons I do not
have to love their father.
All the beds of their
begettings now are gone.

Sincerely.

River Poem For Morgan And Rorie
on the occasion of their marriage

One evening this summer, just at dusk,
two black ducks light on the rocking dock.
They are, I think, taking a break
from rough water and rising wind,
sitting, picked out by the setting sun,
comfortable, close and trusting together.

Up in tall grass nearer the house
fireflies begin their evening dance,
a silent show of perfect light
not as random as it appears,
part of things as they are
and have been a long time.

In the still dark before morning
I lie and listen hard as
one loon calls and calls,
flying over, flying back.
At last the other answers.
I can sleep again.

This is all I ask for you --
this staying together
in whatever is, steady
in all winds on all waters,
shining for each other in the evening,
answering one another in the night.

FRIENDS

Leaping And Looming
for Louise

In the middle of their walk,
road closed, manscape abandoned,
they descend to the odd pond,
two middling women in colloquy.
Sudden as Wordsworth's accusing mountain,
a silent erection of rusted crane rises
over the tree line. Regarded across that bit
of lily-loving water by preying mantis
brontosaurus sized, they lunge away.
Then in a Sunday conundrum of reversing scale,
they spring small frogs from the verge,
natives plunging for life in advance
of Kong's grand passage along their shore.
Through muck, beyond cattail and arrow leaf,
they reach the road again,
antic with the stuff of their adventure.
One stops, quick-picking at her jeans,
provoked by burrs, beggar ticks, stick tites --
astonishing particulars from the untouched edge.
The other, gazing massively past toad flax
and golden rod to singular royal aster,
ponders on the urge of things
to get where they are going.
"Life wants to be full," she says.
Sam Patches all. No bands. No bears.
Just the prodigious leaping.
They walk on.
Think of Margery Kempe,
old and sick on pilgrimage,
cavorting sagely.

A Love Poem, After The Fact

Once, without warning,
he put on skates,
skimmed over wilderness ice,
arms out and lifting
right as marsh hawk wings,
clean lines in the gleaming day.
She watched from his kitchen window,
hands dishpan warm in the cabin sink.
A man of moving grace
engraving faultless signatures,
he edged the unmoved lake.
Racing to open the door,
she called through still dark firs,
"If ever I never loved you before,
always I love you now."
He smiled, spun, rose
to mark the air,
came down to carve
the perfect shapes once more.
As long as she would know him,
he would not skate again.

Lost In The Vineyard

Fall, and all
the Vineyard poems
done for this year.
Mine goes back several years
to Oak Bluffs
and a night on the town.

Furious that my lover has come
trysting with his smelly dog,
a spaniel jiggling the springs,
jingling *interruptus*,
I run off, turning
cozy corners blind
until a jazz piano
pulls me through gingerbread shrubs
to porch steps, where I plunk.

Resting on those lines
I tour the islands of my life
until they stop;
then up I spring and on the lam again,
but I am plucked
from the lawn's dark edge
by the player's voice:
"You," he calls, "you,
Who are you?"

Well, I can't tell him,
can I?

We chat in the shadows,
his mellow resonance
a tonic to my mood.
"Come," he says,
sliding with me toward love,

"let me see who you are."
But I slip away.
Under his cottage keyboard
there is bound to be a dog.

To town, to town,
some famous place
where a blind man sometimes
does the blues.
Cornered by my coat,
head down over brandy
I endure show tunes,
then ply him with a drink,
pleading for those rumored chords.
White teeth, black glasses.

"Tonight, tonight,
you tourist bitch,
tonight you get Chopin."

I carom once again
into the seaside town
to cruise the summer lanes
seeking my man of jazz.

Well, you know,
I cannot find that house again.

Learn, return,
face another music.
Sprawl on pullout springs
practicing technique,
playing elementary scales.
No harmonies. No grace.
Note well the price of theory.
Be still until the ferry docks.
Ignore the dog.

Rangeley Lake: The Silence Of The North

In Maine's western mountains,
dislocated again, I send
my senses out: a whir of nuthatch,
a soft insistence of chickadee,
a rustle of motion from a single crow.
No summer oratory,
no dawn conventions,
just survival, and wings rowing
through bitter, brittle air.
Across the lake an important drumming --
perhaps a pileated making a noise that matters,
like the sudden crack and thunder of the ice.
Inside, the stove fire spits and sings
and the dogs, with thump and whuffle,
settle. So does the cabin,
resigned to a season of heaving.
Making a map of the imagined
I begin to arrive in this place.
Then clock and radio begin:
one says death, too late;
the other cuts with surgical precision
into the center of my dreaming life.
Needle spinning, I crash into the night.
Sharp black tips of spruce and fir
pierce the radiance of a weather moon,
pointing the way north again.
Out on the ice, I slow to a murmur
from the circling mountains' soft round forms.
Around the solid lake stirs the turning year.
I hear, in windless branches,
a silent blessing from the steady snow.

Apple Knowledge

Here in the orchard
where the first apple grew,
we spread a blanket by the water's edge.
You speak about your needs,
tell me how another meets them.

Fading late asters, rusty goldenrod,
October grows old.
Down the steep bank
past a cluster of ash trees,
all leaves save the end ones
paired in coupling parodies,
the wide river moves on.

My roots gone down,
not heeled-in merely,
I feel my knowledge now.
We have had a year
and you have stopped
bringing apples.

You offer one this minute,
your loud teeth
crunching another in hand:
I hurl this apple hard as I can
back toward the tree.
Today all metaphors hurt.

I am aware of sweat
under winter in the wind,
slow bees zoning over fallen fruit,
low light glaring off the crazed
surface of the out-going tide.

Mouth gone dark with panic,
I sense the pattern in the signs,
and smell the autumn,
rotten before the ripening.

When Her Old Lover Comes Into The Restaurant Where
At The Moment She Happens To Be Working

"I want you to fix my breakfast,"
he insisted,
and she resisted,
until Saturday nights
were mere preliminaries
for Sunday morning bouts.
"I never fixed breakfast for my husband,"
she said, "and seldom for my children,
whom I loved."

At the festival in the hollow
they stayed in a damp cabin,
cooking on an old camp stove.
She was making money then
and gladly would have spent it,
but he was always close.
When he began to fix her breakfast
she could see the hooks
curled inside the bacon,
infesting the pancakes.
She loped down the gravel road
to a tavern
for a boiled egg
that was only itself.

After the campaign was over,
sniping went on.
He etched on every other cartridge,
"you wouldn't fix my breakfast."
She agreed. She would have
chosen death instead,
dissolving in orange juice,
congealing in a La Brea pit
of sage and sausage grease.

Toasted like St. Lawrence,
she would have endured,
only murmuring,

as did that holy grilled man,
"turn me over, Lord,
for I am done on this side."

So today, when he comes in,
and she is here, working,
we take cover behind the counter
to watch, and to pray.

Crossing

Look at the creeks she has to cross to get
to him: *Pine Log, Scarecorn, Talking Rock.*
Think of the route she follows, the turns

to miss or take toward the center top
of the state, just down from the crazy bend
in the falling run of *Fightingtown.*

It is a coming-back land, they say;
cedar grows tall, wild rhododendron towers,
fern and galax flourish by the two-pronged seep.

His stonework shores the musty house, half
the deck dropping, like the impossible road, down.
"A slight rain," he says, "and you're here for days."

She sleeps, after serious booze and babbling --
the room, like the curried soup and peppered meat,
too hot -- wakes to dawn and the cooling water.

For a long time after she will stumble over outcrops
of memory: sounding water, the haze, the hollow,
mountain names. Imagine the trail back, learning love

and let go in middle-age. She keeps the sense of him
inside, where something like a stone begins to bloom.
Look at all she has to uncross to get home.

New Year's Day On Talcott Mountain
for Harry

Up from cellars of vintage loss,
old griefs rotated, laid down again,
with another new friend in another new life
I climb a gray ridge in Connecticut.
In these woods, on this day, I feel the cold.

Testing half-thawed spores
I learn how open winter
smells of spring. Hearing
the dog mindlessly flinging
nosefuls of leafmold and earth,
I see within the dimness
of diminished sun
a regular surprise of birch.

Abruptly we come into clarity.
Before us, belly-dropping down.
To westward, middle and background
range, dark blue in sudden light.
I'm stunned into color by wedges
of brilliance. Nose down, shapes of sailcloth
wait. Hang gliders. Launching platform.

With helpers steadying guy wires
and straps, in turn they catch
the moment, hurtle self and sail
into space to ride the thermal
up and up in the gathering air.

The Farmington River moves in its valley.
Hopmeadow Road approaches.
Trees mark cut-off meanders.
Fields alternate plowed and green.

On up the ridge, above Hueblein Tower,
gliders drift and turn, orange, scarlet,
burgundy, black. One at a time, as they flew
they fall, not with plummeting
or hawking stoops, but in slow spirals
and side-slipping sway, nosing down

toward a field near the river. Riding in
on precise final glide they land
where their friends are waiting.

We linger to the last, then turn
and hurry down the mountain
toward our own dark road.
Even the dog is cold and tired.

Spring Ride

i

Without camera
we hold this image:
facing the wind
I tie back flying hair
with blue bandana.
Nearby, in God's Acre,
Old South Windsor's burying ground,
thin, upright headstones
stand red and white.

ii

This country is flat and fresh.
Jonathan Edwards,
the Great Converter,
was born here, a preacher
longing for a broken heart.

iii

May, and the big river
over its banks.
Willows stand in water.
Snapped limbs drive fast
downstream against contrary wind.
Shad move against that current
urged by time and season.
Two men show us a landing net
full of fish, heavy, still shining.

iv

Briars line the wayside,
and poison ivy. We keep to the road.
But there are lilacs, light
and dark and white: blooming
later here than in Lincoln's Washington,
where Whitman plucked his coffin sprig;
earlier than in upstate New York,
where I used to grow them

v

Return against the wind,
knees aching from added strain.
I want to collapse, quit.
Breathing, counting,
I reach the highway bridge.
In truth, we have a short ride.
Bikes lashed to the rack,
we measure the route:
eleven miles, all told.

May Day

Early morning
in a second floor flat,
bare gray balcony hanging
over city back yard, monochrome
trees mocking the ground lost.
Alone in the terror of spring
I need to remember Kathy.

She rolled a cone of colored paper,
glue, paste, staples and tape;
scored jonquils and narcissi
from landscaped borders;
tore periwinkle and spurge
from beds under specimen trees;
snapped apple blossoms and japonica;
ripped muddy strings of veronica
and jagged plants of dandelion
from neighboring yards; roamed our
back fields for wildlings from
a cellar hole by the railroad tracks;
poked everything into her basket
and hung it on my front door.
When I opened to that secret garden,
petals of giggle drifted from behind the garage.

At eighteen, you will have bloomed.
I wonder if you ever knew how
your floral *copia* took my heart.
Kathy, I want to tell you,
it is May Day again.
May Day.

Buddy System
for Ruth Johnson

On a day when I am down,
will not smile, will only frown,
I recall, across town
I have a buddy

who understands things --
how life takes as it brings
and then suddenly sings --
that's a buddy.

She knows the ship docks
when you undo the locks,
stop throwing rocks.
She's no dummy.

Not rowdy, not a clown,
she gets the rightness of a noun,
knows a dress is not a gown.
She's a poet;

knows her rings from her dings,
that too much alone stings,
and words have wings.
She's a buddy.

Time ticks, then it tocks,
so when a lumberbeast mocks,
grab your ocelot socks
and be my buddy.

The Harbor Master

This man wants oceans,
wants herons still
against red setting suns
on every westering beach.
He wants to put ashore
on castle hills,
survey horizons,
then sail bare-poled
through hazardous seas
and high, tumultuous risk.

Controlling harbor knots,
monitoring fantails,
he settles for a tidy scheme
of sloops and ketches
measuring their tethered circles
with little rigging sounds.

Here light changes over surfaces.
Children pass, strangers
pausing briefly to be amused.
He remembers himself
a young sailor, "Born to Lose"
tattooed upon a hard, sinewy arm.
Shooting his braided cuff,
adjusting his cap,
polishing his eyes,
he shuffles along
immaculate docks
aligning hoses.

He wants to remember,
he wants to forget,
the moon, the star, the planet,
and slowly opening under him,
the deep green sea.

Alice's Easter Basket

Forty years ago
in another town
I had a friend named Alice.
Some of this is true.

Down boulevards bare as prairies
we pushed our babies to the park
where Chinese elms pretended shade
and fall depended on pin oaks.
In those suspended afternoons
Alice sometimes fed me
bits of her own childhood
in Sweets Corners, Wisconsin.

She rode long hours to school,
pumped gas across the road
at her father's garage.
Evenings, she and her sister
walked around the long, long country block;
there was nothing else to do
and nowhere else to go.

I met her parents already old.
Knowing nothing of their lives
I have imagined their deaths.
Crossing that familiar highway
between house and garage,
taking safe passage as customary right
even in rain, at night,
her father ended end-over-end.
Her mother was so shy
I was never certain
if she were on the sofa or behind it.
I think she just diminished till she died.

Now, when once again warm winds
bite the sweet, fat buds of spring,
I think of Alice's secret, the attic center

of her happiness. Pumping, walking,
bumping to school, she knew.

She knew that up in the still dark top
of the house waited her Easter basket,
certain to fill in the course of time
with chocolate lumps of proof
that something loved her.

She would tiptoe through that solid German
house and, sitting amidst Teutonic trunks
of durable dark brown clothes, on furniture
stiff with horsehair and salvation, she would
touch that fragile woven basket with
delicate possession. It was enough.

Alice, forgive me.
I've made it up and got it all wrong.
Here. I'll trade you.
Imagine, on my mother's closet shelf,
two scrapbooks; one, a forgotten color,
bulges with cards, snapshots, keepsakes --
every page informed in familiar script.
The other, saying BABY
in gold leaf on pure white padded cover,
lies flat and, after two pages, empty.
You take my baby book.
I want your Easter basket.

Birding In Ontario, Autumn 1980

for Annie, Richard and Bruce

It was a day for falcons, still and warm
at the shift of summer. Before the Picton ferry,
buying apples and cider, we looked for
clay-colored sparrows and cliff swallows
adapted to barns, but once on the island,
on new-plowed ground, we captured killdeer
in our scopes, and black-bellied plover. Over us
marsh hawks watched, harriers riding high in migration.

Long rail fences. Silent pastures.
At the old lighthouse on Prince Edward Point,
eating ripe tomatoes with bread, and cheese,
we found neither waterfowl nor shorebirds;
were found instead by merlin and kestrel,
smaller and smallest of the swift sudden order.

Back along a roadside of bugloss and teasel,
in this drought-dry summer's single still wet pond,
we found ducks -- widgeon, gadwall, mallard
and black. Gunwise, they shot up when we
opened the trunk to set up tripod and spotter.

So why were we surprised, far out on Point Traverse Road,
to be caught by a peregrine, the duck hawk? Long gone
from the east, possibly released, she looked to be at home
on tip-tilting scrub cedars in a slowly over-growing field.
Even with our spyglass we could not see what she was eating:
precise, unhurried motions; cleanly marked head; drop,
catch, rise and eat again, the Pilgrim Falcon.

We witnessed there. Then, light and color going from
the short autumn sunset, we hurried to get back home.

Alpha, Beta, Gamma, And So On
Summer Solstice Fragments From A Workshop At Banner Lodge

I.   On our way to Alpha I tell David
       why I dread this time of year:
       my last child leaves to be with his father,
       and my world reverses toward the dark.
       This year and next he will return by equinox.
       I have two years to find more grounds
       for life than being someone's mother.
          All that history, says David. We are
          the ones who said: "Be" "Here" "Now."
       It is not change but dreading
       that brings the panic on.

2.   Up a hillside in a slow tai chi,
       women unknown to me bring summer on;
       hands in prayer shape pointing to
       their hearts they indicate Namaste.

3.   This is the moment when the sun seems
       to stand still. We mark earth as plainly
       as gathered ferns make shadowgraphs
       on paper fading from blue.

4.   This moment is non-negotiable.

5.   This gang, this circle of foolery,
       mark one ground I can root in.
       We trade fragments, joke in iambs,
       try words like "logorrhea"
       and "echolalia." On this day, like eggs,
       we can balance on our ends.

6.   Perhaps somewhere opposing armies
       stop, dazed from wreck and mayhem
       by this amazing light. Here a brilliant
       oriole drives away the radiance of
       a spectrum-breaking crow.

7.   Hearing guitar and fiddle, I move to
       my own devotion; with cloggers keeping
       time, tap and stomp, wheel and turn,
       I circle in circles with Susan,
       as we waltz in the light of noon.

Doing A Turn On Susan's Turning Forty

The way we've set it up
numbers are what they are
so forty it is, -- but the turning,
Susan, the turning!

I forget: is this the moment
you become a woman
of a certain age
or the day time turns on you
and you turn into crone.

It is believed to be
a turnstile moment
with no turning back.
Unlike a turnabout boat
we tack and tack
into a wind that never turns --
no matter how we try to run before it
there is no turn toward home.

I hope you'll turn another way,
turn it inside out and upside down.
Look how you're turning out already,
turning away from the old turntable.

Turn it up, Susan. Let it
burn and shine. Let the
earth turn
while you dance on
in the midday sun.
Now and now and now,
it is your turn.

Kinky And Skew Are Friends

Kinky and Skew are friends.
Well, friends as best they can be.
Like, when Skew decides
to host a luncheon
just for ladies, she says
"Kinky, tell me when
you cannot come"
and has it then.
So Kinky plans a picnic
on her boat next summer.
Skew will come
and Kinky will run out of gas
far from land
in deep deep water
and Skew will suffer *mal de mer*
and up will blow a sudden summer storm
with sleet and hail
and Skew will be so cold
she cannot stand it.
That's the way Skew
and Kinky practice friends.

Kinky And Skew Argue About The Famous Writer's Hair

"It's bad," says Skew,
"He needs a mirror,
someone tall enought to tell
him 'look here, you
look *coiffed*, done up, done over,
this will never do."

Kinky blinks: she
wants to say "No,
his way is rustic;
his abundance is in keeping
with his kind North Country heart."

But, honestly, what Kinky's
really up to is imagining
her hands and other parts
lost in that backwoods bush.
She is talking wise again,
and thinking Kinky.

Kinky & Scary & Corn

Skew's friend Scary
asks Kinky to a party
and she means to go
but first will watch
some fancy dancing
at Schemitzun,
a native-American festival
celebrating corn.

Arranged in teams, distinguished
by their costumes, dancers shake
their fringe and jingles, toss their
crests of unflawed feathers, move
their feet as animals might
while all the drummers drumming
in their rings around the mother drums
are seated as they might be
on the mother of us all.

Each group is better than another
and all of them are best. At last
they all go out before,
a thousand fold,
they all come in again
together, except this time,
alone, there is the One,
the tall, the young, the dark,
the fully-haired, the ripple-armed,
the supple-skinned, the One.

Dancing as triumphant bird
claiming this harvest for his own
he works his high-legged leaping
and thigh-muscled stopping
perfectly to keep his plumed tassel up
and his unblemished feather moving.

Kinky watches until it is
too late already. When she can
stand again, she calls Scary to apologize.
"This is really true," she tells her,

"I could not come to your party
for I have seen the Corn God
and he is beautiful."

Kinky & Scary & Corn: Part Two

Another time, when Scary's husband
asks Kinky to a party, she says "yes"
and this time gets there. Someone tells
about a bunch of women lunching, munching
drippily on corn, and of the quiet one
who told them, in her country, one would take
a small piece plain and pluck each kernel
separately, relishing the taste, making none
of this crunching ugliness and mess.

Kinky and Skew try it, taking turns on a
single piece, feeling foolish and then
enjoying the Zen of it. A camera clicks.
Kinky looks up and there is Scary grinning.
"Let me tell you all," she says,
"the truth about Kinky and Corn."

Later at home, exploring
a new sag in her pocket book,
Kinky finds several small chunks
of shrivelling corn, stowed there,
she is sure, by Skew and Scary.
She laughs, along in her kitchen.
Then, being Kinky, she sighs:
what would she not give
right now for just one dance
with the Green Corn God,
and one whole darkening harvest night
in which to clean with delicate care
one full-size cob for her purse.

Dr. Kinky Sex Plays Wally Ball
for Bill L., who said volley ball this way on purpose

Actually, she doesn't.
She did, once,
didn't like it --
bashed her thumb,
thumped her wrist,
twisted her knee,
knew how it felt
to feel like killing,
called it quits.
Dr. Kinky
likes to think
of all that teamwork --
assists and set-ups,
rotating serves --
but she plays squash,
smashing small
hard balls
off all four walls;
now that's
Kinky's kind
of wally ball.

Memory And Shakespeare
for Susan

"Take back your boxes," she said,
trying to stay my rising whine
against a U-Haul life. "Remember."

Some of them I emptied, others tossed.
The ones too full of trouble, I resealed:
God being good they will store themselves forever.

How I have lurked in my own dark corners.

Driving north to the River, I think
"this is the place," then am helpless
to hold against the shifting slick
of my Iago mind. " *What* is
this place?" The answer comes
as it always did in our Mister Bones routine:
"Why, this is Illyria, Madame" --
and he and I are young and funny
friends in love again.

Sometimes memory is just
a husky rustling, a silver cornfield
in low October sun. Other times I watch
a hawk seek wind on stammering wings
and will the worst of everything
upon him: in my orisons beseech
that he have only boxes,
no light in any room.

Surly And Skew

Kinky's friend Skew and Kinky's son Surly
have a bad thing going. They started modestly,
snickering at exploding Santa dolls,
progressed to savoring tales of Lobster Boy
and his murderous wife and flippers.

Kinky tried not to mind, even helped them
dig out morsels otherwise they'd miss.

Now they're sharing clippings about a man
found in bed with pieces of his fond mother's
corpse. Henry Heepe his name is: he said
"I cut out both her hearts." Other parts
were simmering in a pan upon the stove.

Kinky's stopped the papers, changed the locks,
put grills across her windows. She keeps
the van gassed and loaded. If ever she hears
them laughing together again, she'll be gone.

Misoneism At The Hillstead Museum
Sunken Garden Poetry Reading: Summer 1998

Each time this garden timeless,
a changing voice,
a different blossoming.
It should be Susan here,
and Charles, or David and
Susan and Drew and me.

Under this apple tree,
green blue gray clouds
and the darkening sky,
we always sit angled so.
It used to be Susan and Drew,
or David and Susan and me.

Podium bouquets elaborate
toward posh sabbath shows,
except for the cattails
and Queen Anne's lace.
Where are Charles and Drew
and David? Where can Susan be?

Could be these trees are olives.
I am losing the names of things.
The flute woman plays with a mad
guitarist. All is raw lament.
This night no poems, no blooming,
no Susan here with me.

Or She To Paulina?

You fool, let it go.
History does not matter,
nor should glory stay.
Craving honor just
for having stood and fought?
Old warrior, go find other
veterans, wave a flag.

Your mother was right,
you are too sensitive.
You learned to guard yourself
against drawn weapons,
never to wear protective gear
where you would love.

We always want to think we
sacrifice for those who follow,
then cannot bear it when they
cavort in hallowed places.
Better to turn old battlefields
into playgrounds to suffer sport
and trampling. Thus has it always been.

Come, this embattled stance
ill becomes you. Paulina
will survive without your
tiresomeness. You will have
made a difference, or not.

No other tall man hunkers
quite like Charles.
Down he goes, folding
with custom-made precision
into formal study, and
there he holds, biding
in intricate balance
until the moment comes
to perfect his own unfolding.
Watching through broken mirrors
of a child's plastic periscope
I see the tremors of ascent begin.
Then up and up he rises
zooming through my field of vision
as though his lengthening body were
thruster and missile too.
He arcs north,
leaving me staring at
the cracking of my own green eye.
"Wait, Charles, wait,"
I want to say,
but he is gone.
High over Canadian shield,
wilderness diminishing beneath him,
mountains and uncut timber
flattening into muskeg and tundra,
he is soaring past the arctic,
coursing toward the secret place
from which the northern lights unfold
in icy undulations of pulsating
blue and green and white.

Margaret Batt

Margaret Batt,
no taller than that,
a memory bigger than all.
Reciting the longest
old parlor poems
with solemn face
and pelting pace
she brings the stories home,
brings the old time
into this time,
makes the good time now.
All praise to Margaret Batt.
Oh, yes, and Maggie Batt
writes a fine hand.
Do not forget that.

Mother, Child, Child, Mother
for Naomi

When I was twenty
and you were eight
I worked in my first garden
never dreaming I would someday wish
you might have been my child there
safe to love and putter
amid the smell of May green
grasses in the rain.

Now you are fifty
and I am almost sixty-two.
When you placed your feet
where I could find them until I stood
on my own, you might have been my mother,
safe to touch while dreaming of
gathering blooms in the garden
I am tending now.

Marriage Boasts
for Naomi and Stuart in honor of their wedding

I would walk
barefoot and backward
from Nantucket
to the Bitterroots
if that would prove
my love for you.

I would scrape a cornfield
out of crystal mountains,
raise deepwater sweetgums
in the wild unceasing seas,
if that were what it took
to win your love.

If you were taken from me
I would tear down all the mesas,
pound the Rio Grande to sand,
sing your name up every roadway
until earth and gods and sky, relenting,
brought you back to me to love.

Wild Children

I must tell you, Sylvia,
our brother Ramu is dead.
Clean clothed, callouses
softened off his palms,
he died without telling.

Do you remember him?
Were you still there when he was taken?
He was ten, then, by their reckoning.
I was already gone,
roaming the secret places.

I knew when I first saw you,
the bones, the eyes --
imagined you captured
in the Caucasus, wind howling,
your own throat torn.

As for me, I survived
in the far north of here:
permafrost, tundra,
the nights clear and black,
loon sister sometimes calling.

Ramu went down in India.
Three cubs were with him
that day in Sultanpur.
He fought hard, they said,
net settling around him.

They took our brother from jungle
to the Little Flower Convent.
He escaped to savage
chickens in a neighbor's coop.
His hair was matted; his nails, claws.

They took him to Lucknow,
the capital of Uttar Pradesh,
where Missionaries of Charities
were run by Mother Teresa herself:
our Ramu figured in her Nobel Prize.

Unlike some of us
he was never put on display.
They say he learned to bathe and dress,
but refused utterly to speak.
He stayed ten years, almost.

In February, Ramu failed to respond
at the Prem Nivas home
for Sick and Dying Destitutes,
southeast of New Delhi.
I wish I knew what really happened.

Zoologists from everywhere agreed
he had been raised by wolves:
"Details have never been learned."
I don't know about you, Sylvia;
I have talked too much already.

Penny Dreadful For Jerry

Came once a wild child
I would choose for a slightly
younger brother if we
got to go around again.

He is best boy, but don't think
Peter Pan, he is man
enough to marry, raise his kids
and stay the course with Dorothy.

He showed the best in students,
helped me through my winter's tales.
In the awful moment of my father's death
they came, nursed my youngest son while
I went to find my orphaned mother.

The Devil may not be in him
-- though there was that catapult:
If you came into his orbit, he
could pull you off your balance,
and let me tell you, boys, you flew.

Yet they taught me steadiness.
Until we stood together on
a nighttime hill in Oregon,
I knew passion, never power.
Only when the laughing poet
begged me not to put the stars out,
did it occur to me I could.

Playing The Bodhran Along The Way To Queen Medb's Tomb
(Bodhran pronounced bough-rawn; Medb pronounced Maeve)

When Manus pauses in the lane
and plays upon his drum
cows come.   They come
from all the corners of their field
to test this edge.
Corporal cows come,
peer with such regard
as might have greeted Medb
or brave Cu Chulain
when she was Queen of Connacht
and he the only uncursed
man left to fight
for bull and honor.

When Manus stays his steps
and beats   louder
on his drum,
what spirits lift
and with the last cows
come as summoned?
Who is watching out
when Manus calls
come   come?

Medb herself might rise
up from her mass of stones
to contemplate the uses
of this man who dares
to stand and beat,
beat upon his drum
come   come.

Climbing Knocknarea To Queen Medb's Tomb

Too fat and lame to climb
I lag along the track
with no intention, talking
to myself as I am wont,
wanting Andrea to go ahead.

I hate the shame
of holding others back
and do not care for help.
"Go away," I think, say
only "Do go on. Please
do not wait for me."

She chats,
does not go on.
Such a bitty thing,
hardly bigger
than my ruined leg.
With my good one
I could kick her to the top
or over the wall to cows
if she is so intent
on large maternal beasts.

We go on.
I grump, begrudge
her steady passing
of all my surly tests,
stall and stop,
mutter, stare my
reddening sweat-faced glare at her.
She smiles;
she really does not care
if ever we reach the cairn.

Andrea, my brace,
my cane, my crutch,
how do you do it?
You never argue,
you just stick.
Without a touch,

without a single push or shove,
you lift me up this "hill of monarchs"
and, true hero, get me there
where it is wonderful
to be a woman
and to be on top.

Why I'm Giving Jim The Carved Bear
Steve Has Given Me, Maybe

Dizzy with Guinness
and too much understanding
I follow him
into the clear cold night
to look for foxes.

He conjures one,
      soothes,
persuades it
      to sit just so
on the high stone wall,
poised before the rising
of the full Irish moon.

Island Beach State Park, NJ

Glenda,
leave the crowded house,
go down the shore with me:
see terns and cormorants,
hunt lady crab.
Come,
we will find foxes,
Glenda,
foxes, Glenda,
nine.

Sensei Moves His Teacup

John moves one hand, rotating it backward
at the wrist, raising his arm slowly,
through early morning light, from hipside
of his own long body, arcing it up,
impossibly up, to circle overhead,
then drift around and down, reversing
curve and motion, hand extending into
offering mode, coming to rest, quiet,
at his waist, where his other hand rises
to take up the invisible burden
and outline air upon the other side.

I have traveled hard and far
for my few mornings with this teacher,
murmured "well met" in New Mexico,
in both the West and North of Ireland,
in the Catskills, Kentucky, the cabin in Ontario.
Now we are here looking out
toward the Green Mountains.
Sometimes watching is good enough.
Better for me to practice with him,
seeking my balance, adjusting my attitude.
Sensei moves his teacup, spilling not a drop.

Sensei Surrenders The Cup

Most recently, I followed John
as teacher, mirroring the moves
of his spirited Tai Chi mornings.

Last spring, in Vermont, I tried "Sensei
moves his teacup," lifted by John's
amazing simplicity and lanky grace.

Years ago, in Cambridge, the one across
the sea, tired of the company of dons,
I fled to an open house for spouses.

Glenda's accent lured me to her.
We bloomed as neighbors, then as friends,
in the housing estate of Chesterton.

John was on sabbatical
for Shakespeare and Psychology:
I had a grant from Trinity College

to finish a book on Dorothy Wordsworth.
In fact my youngest son and I
did explore the Lake District.

Scuttling about in my baby Fiat
we found light in Dorothy's Moss Hut,
epiphany in tiny Dove Cottage.

But, mostly I fell apart. Panic
attacked. It kept me out
of libraries, almost out of air.

Glenda came to do yoga, afternoons.
We had bicycles, sons in schools,
and shared the backs, sticky buns,

book stores, Budgeon's pâté bowls,
and the sports center, where, handicapped
and stubborn, I won beginning women's squash.

The three of us talked lit and psych,
while my son and I feasted on kindness
and Kentucky Brown sandwiches.

We even stuffed all of us into
that little car to share a cottage
for a weekend on the far North Sea.

And I can still see John, laughing,
punting with the tallest pole
under the bridges along the Cam.

Following my family trails, I came
to Berea, where, somehow John, Glenda
and I became each other's teachers.

After that we met when we could,
journeying in every possible way.
I stayed with them in New Mexico.

They came to my St. Lawrence River.
And John was more open and loving
every time we met. The last time

I led him was in a workshop on
"Fearless Aging." He stayed with the trip
through psychic pain and danger to its vision

of death and beyond. I want to believe
that journey helped him when it came
his time to make the crossing over.

Now the force that moves us
has taken away his cup, gently,
and he has gone to rest.

Until we meet again, John,
ten thousand waves,
ten thousand, thousand waves.

Leaning

You need the scene to understand the act
and all the background story for the point,
a book of photographs, a full memoir.

She bends her head for just one moment
to the rough shoulder of an aging friend,
abruptly longing, not for this man here,

nor the former husband, nor the father,
but for a spreading copper beech
or a mottled, solid sycamore.

Safer Love

Swirling green and white in
an arctic blue-black night is safe
for me, for love, for admiration.

Like all poets, I appropriate,
trying, as the rabbi says, to
repair a breaking world or heal

a wounded heart. I surprised
myself saying yes to you
just before you disappeared.

I was born with both eyes open:
I should have seen the casual in-
difference of your philosophy.

Pray I wander consciously
into the loneliness of days
and care a special way no more.

Like the holy one now feeding
birds and gracing gardens, I
would be an instrument of peace.

Louise And The Alzheimer's Screen

This time it truly is her fault.
She is the one who read or saw
the testing, heard the roll, remembered
...Red......Oldsmobile......Cabbage.

Wherever we two stand, sit,
walk or gaze about, we each
recall the other. Now we're also held by
...Red......Oldsmobile......Cabbage.

First thing, each morning, I check my list:
name, date, day of the week,
present location, obligations and now
...Red......Oldsmobile......Cabbage.

No hope before the last memorials.
Our children will set free white doves,
poems, arias and paper inscriptions of
...Red......Oldsmobile......Cabbage.

Solstice

My friend Thia, pushing
back her sun-colored hair,
tells about a four-year-old,
deaf, who will not sign.
They share watermelon.
Thia makes eyes and nose
of seeds and a smile of rind
on her round yellow plate.
Breaking the grin, the child
places mottled rind precisely,
shaping great green ears
beside a speechless face.
Small hands making circles
balance one upon the other,
he moves the top one just
enough to form the sign for "hard."

Margaret

She lives alone,
the only sound
blossoms falling,
Christmas amaryllis,
forced forsythia.

She loves the sun
warm around her shoulders,
wishes it might whisper,
whistle like the wind,
shout, roar.

She walks along
the shore listening,
pauses by the pond,
sees a wild swan feeding
in the dusk, mute.

The Widow's House In Florida

Rooms silt up,
louvers cranked tight
against light on the lanai.
The widow's collapsed,
gone north to live in cold,
clear-headed Ithaca
with her son
and his second wife.
By and by, the son
will retire south
to this tract ranch
on this dredged waterway
scumming over near Venice.
Now, beyond the patio,
where browned grasses crack
pastel cement squares,
hard-leaved trees and bushes
produce a circus of lemons,
kumquats, grapefruit,
and oranges swollen with juice.

Teacher's Pay: Sister Moses

Softly, at the first class you let me know how,
sometimes, the walls closing in, you had to scream.
At mid-term, when neighbors complained,
your sister returned you to the State. You tried
to keep coming, an escort waiting outside.

"Write what you know," I said, as we all said then.
You wrote short poems about patients. I remember
one about a woman who could not swallow: "Get out
of my life, Dorothy, get out of my throat."

When you did assigned description, choosing
the bathroom tub and its eccentric rings,
they stopped your coming, citing deluded poems.

I came to you then, bringing pears and oranges
to share in the common room. You were so dignified
in unironed cotton and rolled-down hose. "Some people
here," you said, "cannot be trusted with hot irons or garters."

Seeing the sleeping room -- sixty beds in rows three feet
apart -- I feared what else might start to close in, petitioned
your doctor to let you return to class. "No," she said,
"writing is bad for her. It gets her all worked up."

Earlier in the term we had read *I Never Promised
You a Rose Garden*. How hard to write of madness
in language that is sane. You and I had smiled, then, in grave
recognition. Now spittle flew from the doctor's mouth.

Your sister gave me Easter Bunny vases she glazed
in pottery class: white with pink dots. I told you I
would be honored to read anything you ever wrote.

A long time later you sent the story of your mother's
life: love, and death, and the clear lunacy of *shtetl,
pogrom, cossack*. Publishers I tried to interest said
it was too commonplace. Then my own walls closed in.

Your name, also, was Elizabeth. I called you Sister Moses.
"Write," I told you, "what you need to remember."

Resuscitated Kinky Looks For Loving Again

She rode her keyboard over
enticing senior sites
and found one suitable,
she deemed, for hooking onto,
reeling up and in.

She chose the usual clean
well-lighted place for meeting,
guessed he looked okay,
believed his speaking tidy.

She was wrong. She thought
he'd said "come play with me."
Turned out he'd said "comply."

JoAnna Came

We know others will come
and go. We'll go ourselves.
Just now it is JoAnna
leaving and I will remember.
I will not forget.

Into a dark year
JoAnna came. She
brought light, laughter,
the gift of competence.
She fit around me like
a shawl, like a comforter,
with the steady arms of a friend.

Driving On

After that hard rain around Utica,
after we had turned north,
the van, the SUV, and me,
we climbed toward the plateau
until we met, one after the other,
two Amish horse wagons, drivers
upright, eyes front. We trailed them,
the van, the SUV and me,
all the way up the North Country
to the top. Finally, in the widening out,
where it seems no one is, we passed
them and the peeling off began:
SUV into military housing:
van hard left into the supermarket
south of Watertown. The old gang
breaking up. I drove on to Canada.

ODDS

St. Lawrence River

Across rough water
a river town
breaks the flow of islands.

Foreground of reeds,
tasseled, swaying
in arrangements of rock.

Dark night and water.
Reflecting on nothing
navigation lights flash.

Being At The River

If this is it
this will do nicely.
Today, with blasts of rain,
wind as unrelenting
as a leopard's eye.
Last week clouds
in fractal layers
mirroring land in mists
of foreground, middle, back,
diminishing in grays
into what looks like infinite.

To get here I was glad,
being on the road
again, though I really
hate driving lonesome
valleys by myself.
Hearing the Kingston Trio
wonder where the flowers
went and when we'll ever
learn puts me at risk.
This nation makes too much
of going it alone,
waging war just to make
us seem like heroes.

Let this be enough:
heron standing on
the solitary rock,
lichen ochre in
the lowering sun, three
ospreys careening up
in widening forays,
that old pine lying still,
root driven into granite,
shaped in bonsai where
it fell who knows how long
ago. While I am here
and when I have gone,
please gather at the River.
I'll know I am not alone.

Kinky Broods On Being Loony

My not wanting
what should not be
disturbs my harmony.
I do it to myself.
That slap, slap, slap
of wings on water --
a deviant cormorant:
I want a loon.

And later when
three slaps are loons,
three loons local
in a clean north wind,
instead of simple pleasure
in the genii of the place,
I spoil my peace with glee
and vindication.

The Martin House

Dear Son,

I'm sorry to report a natural mishap
to your purple martin house, the one
you hopefully installed upon a platform
high up on a tall birch pole.
Its situation there upon the point,
storms being what they are, especially
as we lie facing the prevailing winds,
challenged that birch, which is lovely and graceful
as we know and weak to the core.
Off snapped the top half and down
went platform, purple martin house and all.

Of course, it had never housed a martin,
only wrens, those tiny tyrants claiming
all the local bird world by sabotaging
other nests with early season twigs
and then proclaiming incessantly their triumph
with witchety, witchety, wichety, wichety witch.
At least five wren's nests sit with sticks asunder
where now upon the ground lies the wreckage
of that crafted manse which would indeed
have been a splendid home had martins come.

I've left the shattered ruins where they fell
so this time you can ascertain yourself
that I am not inventing such a sorry
tale or even plumping up the truth,
though I'll admit I do go on a bit.

      love,
        Mother

Raccoons Summer 2004

Max & Henry, Max & Henry.
How many generations in 30 years,
Max, have descended from you, the Matriarch,
and the two young you brought to show us
that summer after the one in which we rescued
you, your mother squashed on the highway?
Poor little Henry died that first summer,
taken one night by a silent owl,
but you, big and smart, followed me
as on hands and knees I showed
you how to wash your food in the River.
You thought that was dumb and gave me
such a raccoon look as I have not forgotten.

We left the island in time for school,
saying goodbye in tears as you tried
to follow the boat. I never thought
to see you again. When two of the boys
and I came up for Columbus Day
I looked around without much hope.
I even called your name that night.
Next day, as we were swimming, off
the shore you came to join us,
biting and scratching in your joy.

The next summer I was here
alone, wishing you would come.
One July night I heard the rustling
grumpy chatter as you ambled
down our path to the shore. When
I said "Max," you swirled, stopped.
You would not approach and clearly
I was not to move. I waited.
At last you stepped aside and let
me see your babies, two, of course.

Off and on now thirty years
raccoons and young have passed the cabin,
never tame and yet not quite
wild. I know never to tempt
with food or garbage and at night

I close the cabin doors in case
ancestral memory stirs and says
"this is our home." So, Max,
I take responsibility
for what happened here last night.

I have company and much
sweet food was left upon the table.
Fresh ant traps, tempting mouse bait.
Porch light on, the door not shut.
In the night I heard the great
commotion, thought it was a guest.
Later when it got too loud
I came downstairs to see
cinnabons ripped from the box,
chunks of fresh hard roll all over,
scraps of plastic bag and oh!
shredded ant traps, empty poison
pellet bags. Beyond the open
sliding screen they curled and tumbled,
cavorting now they had their fill.

I told them I was sorry. Nothing
I could do. Started to tell
them of their many times great grandma
but they had heard enough and sloped
off into the night. I know
they are suffering, will die
in thirst and agony. This may
be the end of your line, Max.
Rest in peace. Forgive me,
if you can.

Kinky's Had It With Raccoons

Kinky's had it with raccoons.
They raid in broad daylight, four
today and butter would not melt
in their cutesy mouths. "This is
our place," they proclaim, and scratch
whatever they please, rip, all screens
shredded, never mind mosquitoes,
lobsters could get in at night to bite.
What became of fear? Aha!
Kinky's the one who feels it now.
That's it. She's off to town today
to buy a gun. Since a shred
of tender's hanging on she'll start
with spritzes of ammonia.
Raccoons! that had best suffice.

Sixteen Questions After Neruda

If I am still hearing Neruda
how is it that he is dead?

And if I am hearing Neruda
is it possible that he hears me?

Why does the yellow dog care
so much about the yellow ball?

If God is everything and everywhere
can She step back to admire Her work?

What do lichen growers have
against purple and blue?

If wind blows hard enough the other way
couldn't I step in the same River twice?

Why willow, hickory, white oak and pine?
Why columbine, cranesbill, pale corydalis?

Who said if I were to stand up straighter
you all would like me better?

To whom shall I return the night's music
when all I received was the bass?

Is God intent upon annoying when
She sends both speed-boats and wasps?

Since herons all seem to be querulous
shall we assume pterodactyls were, too?

Who doubts the mysteries hid
in the red bill of the Caspian tern?

I understand that jet-ski riders love to walk upon the water:
must they then step out upon my private isle to make it?

What is the use of questions?
What is the use of answers?

How do the rocks respond
to the waving River?

When nine mergansers swim into the bay
why ask why and not why not?

Manatee Wannabe

Kinky wants to be a manatee.
Yes yes
she knows they're near
extinction
and have a narrow range,
but, think,
they have to eat
and eat and eat and eat
and really
can do very little else.
Kinky thinks that's neat.

Earthly Paradise: A Catalogue

Take the day as it comes with *le petite déjeuner*
egg cups in blueberry blue and white, *café*
au lait bowls, outsize mug if I choose.

One night in a Bloomsbury bed
and I cannot find a shower. Gladly
I dabble in moonshadow fountain stream,
dry with a towel unaccountably left by the sea
on a transatlantic liner's steamer chair.

It seems most effortless here. There are tools;
no one's using them. I see a man
with a spade, one with cordless edger,
one turning compost in a tidy biostack.

I shall step along on terrapin stones,
eluding rabbits of time, shelter in a Monet's
arch, retire to a Lutyens bench by the pool.
Olive and sycamore dapple me clad
in clogs and canvas smock while *cymbopargum*
nardus burns in blue Vietnamese pots.

If the sun is right, my solar fountain leaps.
I snooze until ready for *Provençal* ware
with Lady Grey tea and bread and berries.
Up then for bocce ball and Jacques croquet.

So over the little bridge, past a Kasuga
lantern, we will dine this evening
seated on Star & Dolphin, or Bilbao
with umbrella-friendly cloths. Cabaña
veils seclude us. While the gnomen on
the solar clock loses time we'll speak
of Berkshire, Avebury, Adirondack, Pawley's
Island, Pemberton and Saranac.

This night we'll linger in the garden, sleep
on teak or Antibes double chaise. I shall
thank my maker all night long, for this is
Heaven, nor am I out of it. Praise be.
Blessings on you Smith and on you Hawken.

And While I'm At It

Blessing on the car wash
right beside the Mobil station.
Under safe cover there
of low descending suds I know
once more rotating purity
and all the godliness I need.

A Cynic's Prayer

Dear Lady, please appear
before the people of Hartford;
cause them to lift their faces, hope
for something other than what is.
Give them teams of angels
to replace their patriots,
and bulky thrones to hold
the asses who have managed
this town into the devil's
descending realm. Black locust --
thorny locust -- what does it matter?
Dear Lady, please, just come.

Trail Marker

Maybe it was rape.
Hot noon up a hillside
over Chenango Valley
in day's silence,
a walker tramping
switchback trail
up a ski slope mountain
flushes a pair
of filmy bikini briefs,
unweathered, fresh today.

Hard to see the scuffle
in scuffed tan bark. Could
blood disperse? She should
have left sign -- laughter
droppings or crumbs of scream.
This tracker wants only solitude,
shade under oak and pine,
tall grass for a scented bed,
afternoon long and fine.
Maybe it was not rape.

Transit

All roads dark coming
into North Egremont,
new moon's skinny arms
lug the old moon on.

Time slowed already
she braces not to swerve,
young buck running at her
toward the light.

Neither stops, the beast hits,
clatters, spins off into black.
Front end smashed, stop
may never go again.

Old woman after this night,
only young remembered
arms drive her south
out of Egremont.

Me And E. Annie Proulx

Bunny says
she sees a white dog.
They all say
no, you don't,
calm down,
take this,
you'll be all right.

Years later
when they come upon
the white dog's tracks,
or see the dog,
or find the dog's white bones,
they say,
how did you see that?
How did you know?

Meantime, Bunny
smells something dying.
They all say
no, you don't,
calm down,
take this,
you'll be all right.

Schizoid Progress

Other times
the ceiling opened,
the roof split
and the watcher warped into distance,
until earth was smaller
than a tiny eye
and there was no sound.
This time the ceiling holds.
At the base of hundred foot walls,
the child sprawls.
She thinks she did protest,
smashing her head,
jiggling her hands,
like toys, in a lark of motion.
The watcher cannot remember.
When the child twitches,
the watcher creeps a bit higher,
then settles, feels a little,
feels a little sorry
for the rucked-up child.
After a long time
the watcher drops
small
hard
words
which hit
but do not move her.

Raptor

Give those other hawks
to Yeats and Hopkins,
I want this one winging
now over our monument
to Daniel Webster and
our irregular town green.
The bank says 97 F.
Thunderheads are mounting,
riding one another higher.
Still she soars above
the gray green of trouble,
up to postcard whites
puffy against true blue.
I could have faith
in the possibility of her --
pulling our outcries
toward convergence,
dropping habit and
the all the same out
of her perfect curve,
knowing she notices,
believing she sees.

Etheldreda Of Ely aka St. Audrey

You need to remember this. Etheldreda
daughter of a King,
lived and died a virgin.

Married off to Tondberht in a real estate deal,
she got her dowry back
when the old man died.

At home on the Isle of Ely, again for political reasons,
she was forced to marry
the boy king of Northumbria.

Alas, young Egfrith grew to want more from marriage.
After some unpleasantness
Etheldreda became a nun.

In the year six seventy three she restored a church
and built her monastery
where Ely Cathedral stands.

Try not to think about the rest, her disinterment,
witnessed by Wilfred the Bishop
and the physician Cynefrid,

the tumor that had killed her healed, her body sweet,
the grave cloth fresh.
No question she was a saint.

But before, when the tumor grew upon her neck, they'd called
the punishment divine,
for she'd worn necklaces,

and everybody knew that tumors grew from vanity.
In fact, she died from plague,
as did her sisters, nieces, aunts.

Never mind rich bishops, reformations, battered shrines,
the hand found in Arundel,
or the relics stored in London,

before she was St. Audrey, she was Etheldreda,
the Abbess of Ely. Yet
when her feast is celebrated

on the twenty-third of June, they set up stalls
to sell cheap necklaces
that thus are known as tawdry.

Grafitti Amongst The Ursulines

At a Women's Literature Conference
at a Catholic Women's college,
she excuses herself, only to find,
neatly on a restroom cubicle door:

> *Lord, I thought I had you.*

Accustomed to Priapus and Venus
engraved in public sport, she looks again

> *Met God in the ....*

In the ?? In the morning before her roommates' rising
drove the sisters' whispers from her ears?
In the night, the city silent, light leaning on the window bars?
Or in this place of meditation where she sits, searching the word?

> *Please, dear God, let me finish my term paper on time.*

Ah well, no exaltation here, merely a settling for terms.

> *I love big cocks!!!*

Thus it is we all come to deny the contemplative life.

> *Let there be peace to all good men.*

She hopes what defines the goodness of these men
will not be pieces of all good women.

> *Please flush twice. It's a long way to the cafeteria.*

Ahhhhh, students. Comfortable once more with the familiar, her own
cloacal vision purged, if yet unredeemed, she returns to the conference.

Later, in the airport LADIES, she learns that

> *Angel wanted to love Bobby until she died.*

Angel, Angel, settle: Bobby wants to love God.

Panopticon

Or Nuts To The Sons Of Abraham
A Nod To Jeremy Bentham
A Bow To Jeffrey Rosen

When terror is the familiar there's no room
for more. Only particulars vary;
planes, parthenogens. Surveillance, too,
a constant, only the watcher changes.
Conceive a child chased in utero
by the finest, sharpest needle made for knitting.
If she survives, she'll always know that life
is what is accidental, death the point.
As for that state of conscious visibility
meant to induce in inmates an unquestioned
permanent faith in unverifiable power,
which old man with a rule book do you mean?
Allah? Jehovah? God?

Dr. Waller Thinks Of Kinko's

Kinko's keeps it up all night --
thrumming, thumping --
all that equipment
going all the time.

Dr. Waller doesn't mind
waiting in line at Kinko's.
Attention, when it comes,
will be just right.

Is what you bring too small?
Kinko's makes it bigger.
Anything too large?
Kinko's makes it fit.

Sometimes alone at home,
stopped in the still suburban dark,
Dr. Waller thinks of Kinko's
and then begins to move.

Kinky Cannot Get Too Much of Kinko's

It is always twenty-four o'clock
at Kinko's.
OPEN OPEN OPEN
all the time.

Kinky goes to try the papers:
pastel salmon bedded
on cardstock emerald;
pastel lilac arranged
against a spray of goldenrod
and cardstock electric green.

Whenever Kinky wants
she can shake off millstone,
rub all over with whitestone,
and soak in a mix of sea blue
and cotton acid free.

She can wrap herself
in natural parchment,
follow the bright white wove
to come at last
to the place of lunar blue
and what lies always waiting --
the creamy ivory laid.

160

Kinky Whitman Kerouac Nelson
Sings The Kinko's Information Highway

Should she need to leave the country,
Kinko's Instant Passport Photo
puts her once more on the road.

Wherever Kinky wants to go,
Kinko's has her covered.
Clearwater, Eau Claire, Fairbanks, Abilene,
Eden Prairie, Vestal, Broken Arrow, Clackamas,
Wauwatosa, Dublin, Agoura Hills, Greeley,
Ypsilanti, Florissant, Coeur d'Alene and Skokie,
Tuscaloosa, Tallahassee, Kenesaw, Kahului,
Blacksburg, Whitehall, Auburn, Baton Rouge,
Green Bay, Bowling Green, Greensboro, Greenville,
everywhere is Kinko's, Kinko's everywhere.

Dr. Waller Thinks Again On Kinko's

If Kinky Waller married Mister Kinko
she would turn into Doctor Kinky Kinko.
Then, if marriage torqued his appetite
so that feet, her feet alone,
tuned his hummers to their peak,
she would become kinky Doctor Kinky Kinko.

Then if Mr. Kinko chose to wallow
in the mackerel crowded sea,
she'd warp into stinky kinky Dr. Kinky Kinko.
Dr. Waller thinks this is unthinkable.
When Mister Kinko calls
she tells him "I don't think so."

Fickle Kinky

Kinko's has turned rushed and dirty,
offers no more creamy laid,
so Kinky dumps him.
A short afternoon
with Sir Speedy,
a longer fling
with Mister Pip,
now Kinky's keeping time
with Minute Man.
Nothing to write home about
but he's clean
and gets the job done.

A Capitol Trip

In Washington always
they make new museums,
history and art, of course,
and wars, and wars, and more
wars. Here is one
for weathervanes. Watch
them swivel, swerve about
all which-a-ways to find
the way the wind will blow.
They line up, point the same:
look -- a Lieberman, a Dodd!
So far no Kennedy, and
never a Wellstone, no.

Non carborundum illegitimi

Easier, now, to slide toward despair
or to my father's despised, cynical shrug.
My old flame-full rage is flickering,
scarcely enough heat to keep my vitals

warm, light my limping way to the green
where gather yet again the small town faces,
home-made signs holding the corners.
I slowly wave my little flag, taking it back.

Maybe we actually mattered way back then.
Perhaps we make a difference now.
Hope might not be necessary, or faith.
Just stay stubborn and, yes, refuse to quit.

Amtrak: Riding To Another Protest

From trains we see the backs of things,
derelict America halted along the sidings.
Yet these abandoned stations show
a different way it was -- colored glass
and brick, a sense of ought-to-be.
All the underbrush, creeks and willows:
nothing is tended beside the tracks.
Sometimes a path follows along
the right-of-way, then trails off into the woods.
Here a brownstone building, one glimpse
of a great model ship sailing a balcony rail.
Before I can think "wait," "stop,"
we slide through rocks holding eroding banks,
pass a swamp where one enormous maple
lies uprooted by our recent winds.
And then here's gingerbready Wallingford,
Scotch pines shielding town from the likes of us.

Pythagoras And The Bean Stalk

I am not not surprised Pythagoras
would eat no meat.
He had learned in Egypt
of wandering souls
going round and around again
to get it right: the lamb
you sacrificed might
be your mother.

But did you know Pythagoras
would eat no beans?
The hollow fava stalk
holds the route for spirits
traveling up or down:
tamper with the plant
and you could alter
someone's destiny.

Like others living on the margin,
Pythagoreans came to be
the butt that jokers kicked:
first pushed aside for eccentricity,
then shunned as more than mad,
these vegetarians ultimately
were rounded up
and hung as heretics
to cleanse the body politic
and purify the state.

These days, of course,
we grow more tolerant,
making nutritional pyramids
of beans and vegetables.
Most of us profess
at least a piece
of the Pythagorean
creed: the sum
of the squares

of the lengths
of the sides
and so forth.

The catch, as Galileo
tried to teach us once,
is not who will
or will not die
for what
but who will kill.

A New Man From Marlboro

After the contra dance,
tired out of her mind,
she dreams she goes to lunch
with Paul Newman.

He smokes.
He wants her to smoke.
She wants him,
but not enough to smoke for.

When she goes to the bathroom,
the kitchen workers
spray her with water.
They are jealous about Paul Newman.

He is nice. Tired.
Worried about his work.
They leave together,
comfortable as companions.

When she wakes
she is surprised to find
herself
still not smoking.

Oh, No, Not Another Dream

The man who owns this place keeps
his tools magnificently oiled,
tends land and buildings tenderly.
The other man brings people here,
busses full, all different ages.
I am struck by their ingeniousness
at baby-tending, little mammals
everywhere, all attended to.
I am loving each man hopelessly,
loving the babies, loving the ones who tend,
loving the water, the river and the sea,
loving the gardens, the fields, the distant hill.
Wandering the necessary road,
I wonder why I am here,
loving and longing and living alone.

A Prayer For Late Abundance

Walking in the garden
musing on that nun,
the one who teaches art

appreciation on
the telly, she who praised
the painted "lovely, fluffy"

pubic hair, I think
of Mother and her crony,
Lillian, chortling at the joke

about an old woman sighing,
saying "gray, hell, them's cobwebs."

Gentlemen doctors shaved us
'til great burning bushes
dwindled into scraggly twigs

or vigorous lovers rubbed
like underpants worn
to ward off judgment at

the scenes of fatal accidents.
Age grabs handfuls,
stands aside, whistling,

while the holes dry up.
Lord, have merkins on us.

Webster's Third: "merkins -- false hair for the female genitalia"

Kinky Rubs Plums
part of the long saga of *vagina dentata*

When Kinky rubs plums,
she prefers two,
soft and firm
and that peculiar color.
It takes practice.
Tricky to bruise
with perfect pressure,
softening centers,
keeping skin intact,
so that when the great
toothed mouth approaches
juices are ready to spurt.

Kinky Rewrites Fairy Tales:
The Princess And The Pea

We should not have come.
His idea, really, to trick
them of the family jewels.

That pile of mattresses
was a put-up job;
it wasn't the pea
kept me awake,
it was the missing prince.
I cannot sleep
unless that little rooster
crows for me.

We were fine before,
the two of us,
peeling oranges in the afternoon,
licking juice from chins and fingers.

It worked for them;
they are enchanted.
Now each night
when he has scaled
this height of ticking
he is too fagged, he says.

I know what's happened.
He thinks nothing
will be good enough.
My bier of bedding
keeps on rising
and I will never sleep.

Horoscopy

While fully present in the noticing
I see a pattern in the drops
still clinging to the wire mesh
along the back garden. And then

I think, "with dew my fence is laden,
and yet the rain will not come."
It's gone. Perception muscles in,
strutting before the fence, the dew,

the garden and the noticing.
Yesterday my horoscope
warned that my true adversary
would always be self-deception.

Rather, I think, it is the way
I think about how I think.
Today my horoscope intends
to give me hope of inspiration

"not by God but by a wild
boy portraying Her." "Celebrate
Yourself." My salvation lies,
I think, in yellow butterflies.

Assembly

One crow
calls up morning,
calls calls calls.
Sun rises.
Clouds move.
Faint skunk warns of
something somewhere.
One crow
calls calls.
Light corners webs
on wire fences,
each crystal foretelling.
One crow calls.
Three crows. Seven.
Twenty.

Mephitis Mephitis

February starts so much --
owls, long shadows --
I should be philosophical,
Lowell-like about the delicate
stompings and garbage-
wedging heads. Instead
I dread their digging under,
pungent screwing, fear they,
like roaches, crows and rats,
will come to flourish
in amongst us.

When I call authorities for
aid, they say they have to
trap and then destroy. No.
Send them into fringy woods
beyond the highways. And
do not loose the dogs.

Aubade Longer

She knew
she was in trouble
depending
on the tree --
first glimpse
each morning
out the little window
under the eaves,
articulate,
rose-gray
in winter dawning.

To notice
hastens demise;
attaching
assures it.
Heaving over
she will not
look again,
only stare
at her unmoving
clock.

Panther On The Blacktop

Your town
or other,
red sweater fall
or down-stuffed winter,
that child you see
in the school yard
you think, "ah,
happy time";
go closer.
You'll find light
regarding eyes,
lifting lip
and sleek bright teeth
come spring.

Light In Late April

Was there ever a green
like this one come
at the end of April
with the first black thunder?
Sharpened willow curves
pierce my eyes
naked to all that light
before the dark,
but the grass,
my word,
the grass.

Long Walkers

to the memory of Frederick Moore, Jr.
who acted from conscience

Age and understanding
weaken her knees, still
she stands for the long walkers.
Not the trust-funded
otherwise unproductives
running ridges or climbing
highest mountains, nor
the one-time messengers
racing twenty odd miles
with news of victory or
defeat, falling dead
or being shot. Not even
those massed through cities
or crossing a state together
for a right, a wrong, a creed.
She means the long, long walkers;
a really old lady stepping
twenty miles a day; an appleseed
dropper; this lone communitarian
sitting down to start the sixties
and then walking on.

Rumination Minus the M

I do not understand
how a certain light
glinting on one particular bay
becomes the only light
upon the only bay that matters.

Is it truly just the mattering
of Being   Here   Now ?
What of those other bays --
Naples, Lesbos, Isle of Man --
where I stood stopped in wonder?

Now I possess my soul
in wondering, making certain not
to lose my self in being present
when steely light pricks greening points
to rise and die again in Dead Fox Bay.

News! News! News!

Dorothy Wordsworth would shout it out:
"News! News! News!" It did
not matter old or new as long
as there was news. Of course by then
she had retreated to places in
her mind where she could not be found,
so last year's chronicle served as well
and comforted that ranging spirit
which had climbed the fells and walked the lakes
and made of home a haven for him
who would be famous.

Here at the River I often think
of her, my morning comforting with
tea and papers, old indifferent
from new. Anything I did not know,
or had not thought or always knew.
Something of each expressed in style
I cannot master or already
have and even better. Grant's
dying house now razor fenced:
the brilliant Frick now dead. I want
to read about it. News!

The Permanence Of Unfinished Stories
Star Runs Up the Hill...

In a broadcast on public radio --
the show considering all things --
a live report on sheepdog trials
tells me *Star runs up the hill.*
Her handler whistles:
sheep shove from the pen.

Star shines. I am sure of it.
Well-fed, trained, groomed,
her tireless legs reach for more ground,
alert for reversing signals,
or motions from the silly sheep.

Will she lose sight of the point?
What if her handler dreams
or ewes balk for lost lambs?
This year's grass could sicken them.
Wool growing in might itch.

I lean closer to the receiver,
realize that I am late already
and must myself now run.

Off I go to whatever demanded.
Now, for me, somewhere
up and on and always,
as long as I can remember
Star will run up that hill...

ENDS

Sailing Against The Wind

Ashore,
the ruddy turnstones
peck and lift, peck
and turn the pebbles
seeking what it is
they need to live.
What they find,
they eat. Then they
peck on. If
they do not find
they still peck on,
turning stones
until they turn
themselves
to bone
and feather,
dust and clay
and stone.

Sea Glass

Thrown overboard
that old bottle
bottom piece,
rounded square,
whitest green
no yellow in it,
rolled over, thrust,
waved back and forth,
changed to this
salt silvered light.

Forsythia

Abundance of shrubs
along the highway,
civilized here,
not, like laurel,
wild in the woods.

Find the word for
such putting forth;
frond, wand, fountain.
Bend it to the ground,
it will root and
shoot up again.

Beyond New London
low reds of osier twig,
highs of maple bud,
off-white amelanchier
and chartreuse willow
throw color over winter's
leafmold, bark and rock.

Still, the brightest outburst
in spring's uprising must be
these sudden masses,
this yellow-blooming bush.

Corvidae

Out her west office window, late
these winter afternoons, she sees,
beyond scraggly city trees, the day-care,
and the temple dome, endless flights
and shadows. Circling or streaming, she
cannot tell, trusts their rowing wingbeats.

Outside the local hardware store
she loiters a long, cold time, listening
to their clicks and glottals, gawking.
Even knowing they mob predators,
she stands, unafraid, bare head
tilted back below the black flapping river.

One morning in a trick of eastern
light a single crow strutting
on a stockade fence casts
huge menace on her dining room
wall. In an arc of devastation
crow shadow pecks at doom.

If she is lucky, they will last
her time. She will stand again
in first snow in a small parking
lot behind a local store
while masses fly over in a
gathering dark. She wants that.

Doc Watson's "Last" Trip North

Picking fast and clean
the way he taught us,
he sits quiet, steady
as ever, straight up
and blind, one foot
pumping time on
high hill ballads
and long time blues,
the long time,
son gone,
long time blues.

The Futility Of Accumulation

Of course they will praise her
though they will not know her then,
digging, sifting, screening for artifacts.
Wait. At that point, if dating
should continue and time still count,
there will be six dimensional
scanning and subtle vacuums
to handle nuclear dust or spores
and microbes -- whatever
takes her species down.

Say they would have praised her for
her keeping ways, the printed matter
she had clipped, marked, stacked
in boxes, everything of interest
to one particular kind
of twentieth century mind.

Experts could foreswear hegemony
to see the stuff involved in raising
four representative sons, decades
of things that touched what humans
called the heart, the hypothalamus.

And the domestics!! Commemorative
boxes of single buttons, uncountable
jars of screws. Researchers would have gathered,
read careful papers to each other under eye-impairing lights.

So say it might have mattered or say it does
not matter, it will not matter. Just bury her.
Or burn.

Sanibel Island
At An Audubon Society Lecture And Slide Show

From the front, light screens a web in perfect beads
of morning condensation. She sits in back
watching, recalling the barrier beach of that
South Florida island where she once stood feet
deep in shells in opalescent dawn.

The photographer's thinning voice picks its way
along the rays streaming off the beaded
screen, now showing human forms stooped
to probe for specimens; it is as though
she hunched among them as they flocked
like sanderlings tugged by the changing sea.

Here, there and back then at once
she moves through the bayside refuge
seeking storks, egrets and herons,
female mergansers in feeding frenzy
by the outfall along the dike.

Here is a watchbird watching a watchbird;
here is a watchbird watching her.

Still the slides click on, in synch with a tape
of golden strings; sea-grape and gumbo limbo,
swamp pink, white-topped sedge, smooth-billed ani
and the rare avocet. Condominia tilt the island's
causeway end, stalk the beaches, creep along interior roads.
Lured to nest by telephone poles, thirty pairs
of osprey crowd a mere eleven miles.

The cameras move to the dike road to snap tailgating
tourists, passionate with martinis, ritually oohing
at spoonbills, pink and predictable in evening routine.
She tries to see human havoc natural as red mangrove
packing detritus around its roots, extending the bayside shore;
or strangler figs choking the native cabbage palm.

The experiment is not working: self-consciousness
does not preserve; watchbirds do not save.

A sunset shot, wings massed above a mauve
and sepia sea: the old man's cheery call --
"I'll see you on the dike." No, she thinks. Not.
Then fears she might sit there alone
forever, trying to see in the dark.

Natural History

With white tipped ears the squirrel,
bigger than the younger one
with bushy tail, is familiar
in this yard, gleaning feeder
scatterings from jay and chickadee.
Now the smaller squirrel moves
to the pole, lays luxurious
tail over its back, charges.
A woman keeping watch
from over the sink, sees past
her window garden succulents
to midwinter ice and gray,
calls "Look" to the other room
where a younger woman reads.
"Oh, look, the squirrels are fighting."
The younger woman turns a page;
"squirrels do not fight," she says.
Tips escapes up a fence post,
waits. The older woman watches.

I'm Telling You

No, not the barnyard
domestic fowl: it is
the farthest south
Antarctica's blue
iceberg and precise
black and white
chinstrap penguin upon
which everything depends.

Doris Betts And The Four-Leaved Clovers

From the Bates College collection
it comes on inter-library loan, heavy,
mildly yellowed, Doris Betts' first novel.
Taking my winter cold to bed behind storm
windows, puttied sashes, radiators cranked up
to clank and comfort me, I open to her world
of piedmont Carolina, love and risk and
Godwin's cancerous throat, trying to tell
a story when it is already too late.

Stuck to the first page, brittle,
still peculiarly green,
a four-leaved clover.
I pry the long stem loose,
salute the life that pressed it
twenty-five years ago,
and begin to read.

Just as I have Asa, Miss Clara,
Lady Malveena, the dead Jessica
and her boy, Fen, identified, another
clover rustles out, falls to pieces on
my bear paw quilt. Then three in a row,
two on a page, four together in fortuitous
design. I turn pages faster, scanning
this tale, hunting the other I am going to miss.

Someone roamed a pasture outside Lewiston,
or sorted deep grass in a mid-Maine orchard,
reading and picking through how many
long warm afternoons? Against what
trouble was all this good luck stored?

In the end I cannot wait,
turn the book over, lift it, shake
and exclaim at a cascade of clovers,
some landing intact or
sifting down in powdered fortune,
others hanging particular
in the hard, northern light.

Mid-October Morning

Waking to first light,
twin boom roars behind the island,
three sharper cracks beyond the point,
she lies shrouded against the cold,
stunned as sky and water,
thinking of bluebills, mergansers,
blacks. Crows convene. Jays warn.
Loon calls. She remembers hawk's
hover and stare, heron's huge flaps,
gust-driven etching of blackbird flocks.
All that needs to be is here.
Death, then, death to the gunners,
life to the wild-flying birds.

October Meditation In New Mexico

From the van at Bandelier
I rise to greet the morning
one more time.
Not far from this ridge
lived the old ones,
tuned to the constant change
of sameness,
nights, moons, winters, winds
and the still speaking creek.

They had left other places.
We are not sure why
they left this one.
Not so long before they came
Jemez blew, throwing up ash
to flow and drift into
this thousand feet of airy tuff and talus.
The little bits they carved or painted
tease us. How we like to know!
Maybe they used up the wildness
and the growing power of dirt.

Not far the other way
from where I take this morning in,
another big one grew.
Sanctioned by our own elders,
some icy minds used
what they learned
before they understood.

Now every wind brings news
of what they did
and what they plan to do.
We do not know how many
thousand feet of what
will drift and blow upon us.
    Anasazi
    Alamogordo
Names to twine and gyre
until I think to lose my mind, again.

And so I rise in this bright morning
on a blue speck spiraling
to greet this particular
stellar's jay and magpie,
this very coneflower,
rabbit brush and sage,
and thank them each
for being with me.

Kinky Waller Wants To Get It On With The Gift Giver

Possibly named in the Hopi tongue for the desert-robber fly, this Bug-god's nose transformed at length into the Pueblo flute, and he became a minstrel with a back-bag full of songs and a joy in all the ladies.

> You are young, says Kokopelli
> Come and lie with me.
> You are deaf, he whispers,
> Come and lie with me.
> You are small, you are tall,
> Come and lie with me.

He might be the footloose one, the Navajo Hunchback God, with a spear or a wand, or a planting stick and a sack packed with seeds. His most conspicuous potency makes him the Planter God and gives him spring.

> You are dry, says Kokopelli
> Come and lie with me.
> You are a bitch, he whispers,
> Come and lie with me.
> You are hard, you are melting,
> Come and lie with me.

It is said that untried maidens flee from him. Don't count on that. No Casanova of the Cliffs or Don Juan of the Tufa, he is the Dine water sprinkler bringing the People rain and food and life.

> You are dirt, says Kokopelli
> Come and lie with me.
> You are foul, he whispers,
> Come and lie with me.
> You are bitter, you are sweet,
> Come and lie with me.

Some say he was just a traveler peddling wares, announcing himself by flute -- like modern Cobaneros trading turquoise and shells along the Kokopelli Trail. Route markers show him mounted on a modern mountain bike.

> You are a stranger, says Kokopelli
> Come and lie with me.
> You are home girl, he whispers,
> Come and lie with me.

You are found, you are lost,
Come and lie with me.

Knowing sex to be ridiculous as well as sacred, Hopi Kachinas danced in
generous obscenity until the missionaries came and dumped their burden bags of
shame. Now men can only blow on reed and wood and bone.

You are inspired, says Kokopelli,
Come and lie with me.
You are mad, he whispers,
Come and lie with me.
You are cooked, you are frozen,
Come and lie with me.

Kinky wears a likeness of Kokopelli on her ring, left hand, fourth finger.
Constantly, her picto-prayer entreats the universe: If you feel like Kokopelli,
come, be like him. In the spirit of Kokopelli, Kokopelli, come.

You are old, says Kokopelli
Come and lie with me.
You cannot see, he whispers,
Come and lie with me.
You start over, you are done,
Come and lie with me.

IRS

Sorting clumps of papers, hostage
to receipts and cancelled checks,
crooked lines of numbers, estimates
where murk has clouded certitude,
she calculates and ages, faces
what her life is adding up to,
noting its diminishment,
hating its accounts forseeable.

A-Mused

Jordan says you can tell
the good monsters from the bad --
they are still alive at the end.
The young may yet seek one
another's arms. How shall they stay?

I am sore afraid.
One farmer in Japan
held off airport expansion
with a sharpened stick
until old age claimed his heart.

One hundred years ago
Henry James admitted
that his "essential loneliness"
was deeper than his "genius,"
deeper than his "countermining" art.

Mother Grim

No,
she
will
not
pass
this way
again.
Here is
dig,
dig,
cut
and rake,
useless stick
forking
long
evil
root.
What sense
going
over
old
ground?
It all
ends
in tangled
ramblers
and a
rotting
fence.

Our Lady Of Frogs, Salientia

Daily they copulate before her
after the manner of dogs.
Some noons they gnaw each others' tongues,
pleading Her Righteousness
to smite their careless squashers.

Meanwhile their sacred lady sports
outdated pompadour and scarlet
lips, erects three feathers on a side,
strums her unstrung mandolin
and smiles head-cocked without a sound.

Few drivers comprehend the wreaking
of these crouched devotions
when Justice of the Frogs is meted and
in human wrecks on screaming highways
Ranidaen road kill tolls are met.

Reincarnation Plans

When I come around again
let it be as a red-backed
spider. Australian. Female.

If I want babies, I shall choose
one twitchy male and let him take me
hard and long as he likes.   Once.

No sooner have I his cargo aboard
then I will eat him, bite by bite,
thoughtfully chewing to the end.

It is not that I wish to dominate,
nor that I am naturally mean.
It is about survival, sir.

When you were allowed to hang around
in theory helping tend the web,
you did not feed the kids, you ate them.

And that twitching! There the lady hangs,
all filaments aligned and tight,
ready to signal bug for supper,

when stumblefoot arrives, glib
and pouty, wanting whatever it is.
You understand. You have to go.

One mating makes for years of babies.
Young bucks thin their ranks. Champions
take females for a prize. Surprise.

Last Meals
A Rumination In The Hullabaloo Over A Century's Ending

Make mine tea and biscuits, wheatmeal --
the English ones -- right here at home.

Last summer we did not go out
for Bruce's birthday meal and boat ride.
Small black clouds cancel more,
now we are older. It would
have been a perfect evening run,
sun hanging a long red time
over eagle platforms, osprey roosts.

Were I to drown in that great river,
when they brought my body up
it would be hung about with eels.
Lampreys. Call them stone
suckers, for the way they move
rocks in streams, making nests.

Once I made a pot of Twinings
and served digestives to a long,
dreamy man. We had very little time.
After he went back, his mother called.
No more, she said, not again.

They say this world will end
in five billion years when
the dying sun explodes,
engulfing earth. Other stars
have already eaten
planets near to them.
Afterwards, they belched.

Five Billion Years

In loathesome city August heat,
wet lead vice-grips clench her mind
until "This, too, shall pass away,"
"this, too," is all she can remember.

Ice will cease retreating, swerve
forth again; the great St. Lawrence
lose its way, sneak south below
Duluth and drown the Mississippi.

Forget last summer's browned-off
grass. The sun was only practicing.
Time enough to worry when

it makes a move on Mercury,
then spins a little faster, turns
to shine its way toward Venus.

Surmise In Warm December

Did any of those last saurians pause,
with streamers of swampy chew cascading,
and lift a bull whip neck to focus
tiny blinkless eyes on that
approaching chunk and mutter,
warn in flicking hiss, "Here comes the night?"

She wonders, standing in her garden,
both arms tight with deadened leaves,
turning a wrinkling face in search
of darkness, announcing over the fence
in tense mammalian terror, "This time
we shall be dying of the light!"

Deadline

Only cephalopods seem to be
as earth alien as I, especially
in this moment when I must
make a poem or die unjustified.

It is like being bitten by
the tiny blue-ringed octopus.
First a numbness of the lips,
then loss of breath, paralysis.

Right to the end you can
see, hear, and remember.

Outside Heaven's Gate

Here we are,
far colder than planned,
drifting apart, dark,
and not altogether here.

No ship yet,
comet pulling away
ruinous ice upon us.

Black silence.

Where is the ship?
Is there a ship?
But we thought...

Must tell Mulder.

What if
Bo and Peep,
The Two,
not true.

Not true?

Out Of Time

I cannot do a poem for now,
springing from the golden peach of
antique pansies at the garden store
to long black coats and baby faces
in a target school, mounds
of cut flowers blooming
in the slushy snows of Littleton.

Two hundred million years ago
a great eruption blew Pangea, split
the world and let the oceans in. Each
continent slid its separate
way. No doubt, life, as the seas
and the reptiles knew it, ended.

Nocturia

Like a lover comes *Nocturia*
urging me up to show my
constancy. If God made no
demands there'd be no God at all.
You, my true companion, do
return, teach me to mark my hours,
punctuate the sentence of
my life without complaint. In
your service shall I rise, forego
my solitude and move into
the wideness of each expanding night.

Before I Forget...

I was supposed to jot the ideas
for some poems she said she wanted to write,
but you know how she talks when she gets revved?
Well, this is as much as I got:

there was arsenic in his amaretto;
the sinister dextrous man of the night;
kissing toads on Lookout Mountain;
thaumaturgy; and a cat named Spot;

Cassandra ending as a grasshopper shill;
compassion's transformation of spite;
reading newspapers to make sense of life;
some other former century rot.

The rest I forgot...

Anomia

This is not the death she had imagined,
shadows in the valley darkening
until there was no light, or the great leap

after a hostage companion from the span
of a last bridge over a century rapids
into the churning river of cannot go back.

A miserable child, she had seen herself dead
in another culture, flame and billowy smoke
crackling up, over her towering pyre,

while far below, dirt-eating mourners
moaned their failure ever to bother
understanding her enough. This is worse.

A vulture bestrides her, rips away her words.
At lengthening intervals she can still see life
out there in her children's eyes. Otherwise

the clinks and rituals of her routine days
no longer kindle comfort. Language slips.
She sputters, not yet dead, entombed in silence.

Maybe

I have been dreaming
poems in the night,
and feeling helpless
in the morning
when I cannot
retrieve them. Still,
it may mean something
is stirring again.

In my night mind
they sound o.k.

Blowing The World To Peace
Spring 2003

Who would still trust heroes? When Curtis
went to Little Big Horn, Teddy R.
told him: "Keep quiet about the truth."

You, who are you, if you are?
Since we are not allowed to know,
why labor on in this scriptorium?

The naming of the moon -- pink,
sprouting grass, egg and hare,
fish for the upstream spawning run.

On line, the Dalai Lama says
"when you lose, don't lose the lesson."
"Not getting what you want is good."

I have walked nine times about the well,
precise and counter-clockwise.
The cataclysm still comes on.

218

Arara: The Lost Remnant

It turned cold on election night.
Awaiting returns, she learned of the
Arara, an Amazonian tribe declared
extinct in 1950, who re-announced
themselves by killing three government
mineral prospectors in the seventies.
They ate the meat, made music with the skulls.

In the beginning, says their myth,
everyone was a brilliant star
traveling peacefully through the dark.
Then two sons quarreled so violently
the universe exploded. All fell.

All would have fallen all the way down
if it weren't for the giant parrot who caught
and carried everyone he saw back
to the heavens. Arara, the great parrot,
overlooked a batch the jungle hid.

These lost, fallen stars became the Arara,
but they are not the parrot people;
they are the people the parrot overlooked.
They have no hope Arara will return
to claim and elevate them. They know
marauding in the forest, solitary
and alone, to be their certain end.

And so they are the Jaguar people,
painting themselves in jaguar patterns
with a clear invisible sap which
turns dark blue in the light.
Jaguars are the only animals
the jaguar people will not hunt.

Meanwhile, they live together all
in one group. After the men have hunted
and the women have fixed the feast they
have a glorious drunk, make music, and

a lot of love, each man with many women,
each woman with several men. No child
knows its father, no father knows his child.

If anyone eats, they all do.
It is collective heaven while they live
and solitary hell once they are dead.

Of course, Brazil destroys them.
Wapari, the medicine man, who can
appease the animals and birds to sacrifice
themselves for food, and can appease
the earth to produce abundant roots,
and could find haven for the village
when spontaneous fires raged,
cannot appease this government.

"We are trapped. They are on all sides now,"
Wapari says. "We have always lived by the river.
We eat, drink, wash and play together
all our days here. Crocodiles, piranhas,
electric eels -- we understand them. They
bring us no harm. But now..."

He means the giant tree-felling machines,
the slash fires, the earth strippers, the leeching mines.

"We killed the government men because
they are our enemies," Wapari says.
"We have nowhere left to go."

It turned cold on election night.

Kinky Exhorts Canine-Americans

Take over, dogs,
you can do it.
Lock up the meeching
and those soft sad eyes --
use your springsteel haunches,
go for teeth at the throat.
You have nothing to lose
but dull food,
carpet,
and blattey-blattey noises
from that species at the end of their rope.
Do it, dogs.
Do it.

Project For A New American Century

Perhaps they will create an instrument
so fine it can measure things of
no substance, like our president's brain.

The trouble is not that I am too sensitive,
stubborn or impulsive, or that I lead
with my heart, but that, by then, I will be dead.

Found Poem
The Hartford Courant
17 January 1984

Today is Tuesday
January 17
the 17th day of 1984
with 348 to follow.

The morning stars
are Mercury,
Venus,
Mars,
Jupiter
and Saturn.

There is no evening star.

Northern Diver

Cry.   Now.   Loon.

Cry in the night black sky
cry rising out of north
flying over loft,
down point,
no moon to mark your passing
round, around this bay,
a rising tremble
fall of exhausted breath.

It comes to this.

Calling the unknown name
of what you long for
now, loon, and tomorrow
in all the dawns
and darks to come
with none to hear you

cry.

Vincit qui patitur
  "who suffers conquers"

"During the race,"
an almost winning woman, second
in the marathon, says,
"there's no friends."

This one wearing
the quilted face of age, reads
Roethke and Seamus Heaney,
who love their drink.

It's hard to love
a drinking man, especially
a drunken man lying
in your bed.

Bless the moon,
moving away from earth every year
one and one-half inches.
Earth slows down.

Only the moon
has kept earth from wobbling
so we will teeter totter out
eventually.

Johnny Cake,
a little airstrip where once she
hoped to learn to fly, will be
condos, a store.

One prisoner,
accused of writing propaganda,
now silenced in Guantanamo,
was a poet.

FDR
warned, before he got so tired,
against government by organized
money.

There was a god,
a very strange exclusive god,
thought to be the chosen one
in a dark time.

Kinky's Son Solemn Keeps Track of Possible Tombstone Chiselings

She said to go ahead and kill her
For she loved an unfair fight
Now since we would not be bothered
She's gone on and died for spite

Ashes to ashes
Dust to dust
Here lies Kinky
She wouldn't adjust

Water her element
Earth her friend
Spirit her firmament
Fire her end

If one thing doesn't work, try another.

I really liked ice cream.

As long as there is life, there is hope.

Who cares?

Thanks for stopping by.

INDEX (By Title)

230

INDEX (By First Line)